VIDEO GAMES

Other books in the At Issue series:

VIDEO GAMES

Roman Espejo, *Book Editor*

Daniel Leone, *President*
Bonnie Szumski, *Publisher*
Scott Barbour, *Managing Editor*

GREENHAVEN
PRESS ®

San Diego • Detroit • New York • San Francisco • Cleveland
New Haven, Conn. • Waterville, Maine • London • Munich

© 2003 by Greenhaven Press. Greenhaven Press is an imprint of The Gale Group, Inc., a division of Thomson Learning, Inc.

Greenhaven® and Thomson Learning™ are trademarks used herein under license.

For more information, contact
Greenhaven Press
27500 Drake Rd.
Farmington Hills, MI 48331-3535
Or you can visit our Internet site at http://www.gale.com

LIBRARY OF CONGRESS CATALOGING-IN-PUBLICATION DATA

Video games / Roman Espejo, book editor.
    p. cm. — (At issue)
Includes bibliographical references and index.
ISBN 0-7377-1173-6 (pbk. : alk. paper) — ISBN 0-7377-1174-4 (lib. : alk. paper)
    1. Video games—Social aspects. I. Espejo, Roman, 1977– . II. At issue (San Diego, Calif.)
GV1469.34.S52 V53 2003
306.4'87—dc21   2002072363

Printed in the United States of America

Contents

Introduction

On the morning of December 1, 1997, in Paducah, Kentucky, fourteen-year-old Michael Carneal opened fire on a prayer group at Heath High School with a .22 pistol he had stolen, killing three students and injuring five others. According to Dave Grossman, a military psychiatrist and retired U.S. Army Ranger, Carneal fired only eight shots, hitting four students in the head, one in the neck, and three others in the upper torso. "Nowhere in the annals of military or law enforcement history," claims Grossman, "can we find an equivalent achievement." He maintains that "one state police study in an assessment of the accuracy of their officers across several years found that the average officer, in the average engagement, at the average distance of twenty-three feet, hit with 13 percent of the rounds fired." Carneal was not an experienced marksman. Reportedly, other than firing a few practice shots with the stolen pistol, he had never fired a real handgun in his life. However, Grossman contends that the high school freshman played violent video games that trained him how to shoot with fatal precision:

> Michael Carneal . . . had fired thousands of bullets in the video game "murder simulators." His superhuman accuracy, combined with the fact that he "stood still," firing two-handed, not wavering far to the left or far to the right in his shooting "field," and firing only one shot at each target, are all behaviors that are completely unnatural to either trained or "native" shooters, behaviors that could only have been learned in a video game. . . . These kind[s] of video games provide the "motor reflexes" responsible for over 75% of the firing on the modern battlefield.

The "video game 'murder simulators'" Grossman is referring to is the subgenre of video games called first-person shooters (FPS), where players view the world through the eyes of the video game character that they control. In a typical FPS, players wander through a series of halls and passageways and kill monsters, enemy characters, or opponents controlled by other players whom they encounter along the way. Because of advances in computer technology, the animated violence and gore of FPSs have become palpably convincing, immersing players in a virtual world of intense action and graphic violence. The first FPS game, *Wolfstein 3-D*, was released in 1992 by the entertainment software company idSoftware. In *Wolfstein 3-D*, players navigate through the dark corridors of a German castle during World War II and ward off surprise attacks by Nazi soldiers and guard dogs. The game's unique first-person perspective gave a new dimension to the video game playing experience, making it popular among gaming enthusiasts.

A year after the appearance of *Wolfstein 3-D*, idSoftware released its next FPS, *Doom*, which took the video game industry by storm. *Doom* plunges players into a futuristic maze, where they have a first-person's view of blasting aliens with an arsenal of weapons. According to video game enthusiast Darren L. Tabor, *Doom* was immediately successful because it was technically and aesthetically more sophisticated than *Wolfstein 3-D* and had "entered the scene just as modem speeds and awareness of the Internet were increasing." These developments allowed players to connect online and play against one another with ease. The success of *Doom* gave rise to a slew of technically and graphically superior FPSs based on the first-person perspective concept, such as its sequel, *Doom II*, and others such as *Duke Nukem, Redneck Rampage,* and *Quake*.

Although violent video games were criticized after the Paducah school shooting, the question of whether or not they contribute to youth violence became a more urgent matter in the aftermath of the Columbine High School shooting in Littleton, Colorado. On April 20, 1999, high school seniors Eric Harris and Dylan Klebold entered Columbine High wielding firearms, killing twelve students, a teacher, and wounding twenty-three others before authorities found the two boys dead from self-inflicted gunshot wounds. Allegedly, Harris and Klebold were dedicated players of violent FPSs like *Doom* and *Duke Nukem*. A year before the shooting, Harris alluded to these games when he wrote in his journal about their plans: "It'll be like the LA riots, the Oklahoma bombing, WWII, Vietnam, *Duke [Nukem]* and *Doom* all mixed together. . . . I want to leave a lasting impression on the world." In addition, a home video shows Harris brandishing his sawed-off shotgun "Arlene," which was named after a character in *Doom*.

Some commentators believe that the Paducah and Littleton tragedies are examples of how video game violence has lead to outbreaks of real world violence. Education professor Eugene F. Provenzo Jr. contends that violent video games contribute to youth violence because when "violence is stylized, romanticized, and choreographed, it encourages children and adolescents to assume a rhetorical stance that equates violence with style and personal empowerment." Physicians Jeanne Rosenberg and Joanna Santa Barbara argue that "the worst video games teach children to associate violence and killing with pleasure, entertainment and feelings of achievement. As the technology becomes more sophisticated, players are rewarded with more and more realistic depictions of victims going down in blood and flames as they are hit." In addition, Rosenberg and Santa Barbara insist that "children who spend hours improving their skill at these games are not only learning targeting skills, but are undergoing the same desensitization to killing other humans that the military uses to train soldiers to kill."

Others contend that studies have shown that playing violent video games increases aggressive behavior. According to David Walsh, president of the National Institute on Media and the Family:

> In one study of college students, students played either a violent or non-violent game. After playing this game, they were given a competitive reaction time task in which they played against another student. If they beat the other student, they got to deliver a loud 'noise blast,' and were able

to control how loud and how long the noise blast would be.
Students who had previously played the violent video game
delivered longer noise blasts to their opponents.

Some critics are skeptical of such studies that claim that violent video
games heighten aggressive behavior, however. Referring to the noise-blast
study mentioned by David Walsh, for example, Howard Fienberg, a research analyst with the Statistical Assessment Service, states that "researchers found that those that had played the violent game blasted their
opponent longer and louder than those that had played the non-violent
game. But the difference was actually minimal. The blasts delivered by
subjects who had played violent games were longer, by all of 2 percent,
and the average blasts for all the students was about half a second, far too
short for reasonable analysis."

Other commentators dispute the claims that violent video games are
a cause of youth violence, arguing that the vast majority of violent video
game enthusiasts do not commit real acts of violence and instead use
video games to express their frustration and anger. Video game designer
Steve Gibson says that video game playing is "how geeks get out their
competitive spirit because they're not athletic enough to play on the bas-
ketball team." In addition, Henry Jenkins, director of the Program in
Comparative Media Studies at the Massachusetts Institute of Technology,
asserts that the Columbine killers' predilection for violent video games
merely reflected their complex and unhealthy obsession with violence
and destruction:

> Far from being victims of video games, Eric Harris and Dy-
> lan Klebold had a complex relationship to many forms of
> popular culture. They consumed music, films, comics, video
> games, television programs. All of us move nomadically
> across the media landscape, cobbling together a personal
> mythology of symbols and stories taken from many differ-
> ent places. We invest those appropriated materials with var-
> ious personal and subcultural meanings. Harris and Klebold
> were drawn toward dark and brutal images which they in-
> vested with their personal demons, their antisocial im-
> pulses, their maladjustment, their desires to hurt those who
> hurt them.

Because of the senseless school shootings in Paducah and Littleton,
video game violence has become a pressing matter for the entertainment
software industry. In addition to the debates about how the entertainment software industry should address concerns about the violent content of video games, other controversies surrounding video games, such
as whether they can improve children's thinking skills or have artistic in-
tegrity, are addressed in *At Issue: Video Games.*

1

Violence in Video Games May Harm Children

Elisa Hae-Jung Song and Jane E. Anderson

Elisa Hae-Jung Song is a clinical instructor of pediatrics at Mount Zion Medical Center at the University of California, San Francisco. Jane E. Anderson is an associate clinical professor of pediatrics at the same institution.

Video games have become a ubiquitous form of entertainment in the United States; they are behind only television in popularity. For that reason, the violence in video games is a cause for concern. Numerous studies have found a correlation between violent video games and increased aggression in children. In addition, several popular video games may be teaching children how to kill by simulating the techniques used to train soldiers for combat. The skills acquired from these games are tragically evident in recent school shootings perpetrated by teens who were heavy users of video games. To protect children from violence, parents should not allow their children to play video games until adolescence.

Before 1950, books, comics, motion pictures, phonograph records, and radio programs, which included dramas and game shows, were the only media entertainment available to children. Since the offerings were relatively slim, it was rather easy for parents to control what their children listened to and watched.

In the past 50 years, however, children's access to media has exploded, beginning with the introduction of television, which rapidly became a fixture in more than 98% of American homes. The emergence of video games, designed initially as large consoles and then modified for use on home television sets, dramatically changed children's media environment. This new form of entertainment raised concern because the negative effects of violent television on children's behavior had been extensively documented, and video games added an interactive component to the entertainment.

The second most popular form of entertainment after television, video games have rapidly become the largest segment of the entertainment industry, taking in $6.3 to $8.8 billion in 1998, compared with $5.2 billion in Hollywood box office receipts. Video games, which now can be played at home on a computer or a television set, account for 30% of the toy market in America. With 181 million computer games sold in 1998, each home has, on average, two video games.

The time is right to ask the inevitable question: "Are violent video games having a negative effect on children's health?" Although the answer to this question remains equivocal, data now exist to suggest that the answer may, indeed, be "Yes."

Everybody plays

Consider these statistics: About 90% of United States households with children have rented or own a video or computer game, 49% of children have a video game player or computer on which to play the games in their own bedroom, and 46% of children would choose, in preference to any other form of media, to take a video game player or computer to a desert island. Clearly, many homes in America are affected by the explosion of video games.

According to a 1993 survey of 357 seventh- and eighth-grade students, boys spent more time playing video games than girls. While 60% of girls clocked an average of two hours a week playing video games, 90% of boys played for more than four hours a week. Boys and girls also differed in where they liked to play: 50% of boys spent time in arcades, compared with 20% of girls. Only 2% of preferred games had educational themes, while about half had violent themes.

A 1996 survey of 1,000 fourth- to eighth-grade students confirmed that boys spent more hours each week than girls playing video games, with game playing decreasing as grade level increased. Children of all ages preferred games with violent content; boys preferred human violence, girls, fantasy violence.

About 90% of United States households with children have rented or own a video or computer game.

A study of 227 college students showed that 97% of students played games. Again, girls spent less time than boys in this activity. The survey also investigated respondents' earlier use of games: Students reported that the time they spent playing games gradually decreased from the junior high years (five and one half hours a week) to college (about two hours a week). Figures on earlier use of games may not be reliable, however, because they were based on long-term recall.

Parents are usually not aware of the nature of the video games their children are playing. In a 1999 study, most parents were not able to name their child's favorite game, or named an incorrect game. In 70% of these incorrect matches, the child described their favorite game as violent. Even when a parent watches her child playing a video game, she is unlikely to still be looking as her child attains higher levels with increased violent content. On average, according to another study, parents recognized only nine of the 49 most popular video games.

In a study from British Columbia, only 22% of teens said that their parents had set rules for playing video games. This compares with 39% of teens who had rules for television viewing. The rules for video games, when they existed, related to when and for how long the child was allowed to play but did not usually address the content of the game. About 40% of teens had to finish their homework and chores before playing. Only 15% were subject to restrictions on the type of game they played.

These findings are especially of concern because the graphic violence depicted by video games has increased greatly in recent years. According to the National Coalition on Television Violence, a nonprofit organization dedicated to reducing gratuitous violence on television, sales of games rated extremely violent have jumped from 53% of all sales in 1985 to 82% in 1988. Analysis of a sample of the 33 Sega and Nintendo games that were most popular in 1995 showed that nearly 80% featured aggressiveness or violence; in 21% of the games, the aggression or violence was directed toward women. In nearly 50% of the games examined, violence or aggression was directed against other characters, and the violence generally was very graphic. Another survey found that violence was a theme in 40 of the 47 top-rated Nintendo video games. This means that, on a typical day, one of four boys in the United States plays an action or combat game like "Doom" or "Duke Nukem."

The many faces of video violence

Violence in video games can be categorized as fantasy violence or human violence. Each of these categories can be further divided into games where the player controls a character on screen who performs the violence (third-person shooters) or those where the player views the game as if he or she were the character performing the violence (first-person shooters). First-person violence allows the player to actually look along the barrel of the gun on the screen and feel as though he were pulling the trigger and killing someone.

"Super Smash Brothers" is an example of a game that uses fantasy animated violence. The game is rated E (meaning it is for everyone). Descriptions of the game appearing on the package include "Duke it out as your favorite Nintendo characters," "It's a bumpin', bruisin', brawlin' bash!," and "Smash your opponent silly." This game was placed on the "Dirty Dozen" list by the Lion and Lamb Project.[1]

Human violence is the main component of many video games. "Carmageddon" is rated M[2] for mature audiences and is described on the package as "The racing game for the chemically imbalanced." The object of the game is to run over people or crash into other cars. "Waste contestants, pedestrians, and farmyard animals for points and credit," the game instructs players. Points are scored for artistic gore, based on how blood is smeared on the tires after each crash. A player who completes all levels may have killed as many as 33,000 people.

The most popular third-person shooter game is "Mortal Kombat," which is rated M. The package states: "3D fatalities: Watch as brand new and classic fatalities take on a completely different meaning in three dimensions." In 1993, Sega sold a version of the game in which a warrior rips off his opponent's head and spine while spectators shout, "Finish him! Finish him!" Nintendo's version, also rated M, did not include that scene, but it was outsold three to two by Sega's product.

New dimensions of violence

Games that use first-person shooters are increasingly popular. "Doom" (rated M) is the best known because Eric Harris and Dylan Klebold, the Columbine killers, were avid players. The manufacturer introduces "Doom" this way: "A single Demon Entity escaped detection. Systematically it altered decaying, dead carnage back into grotesque living tissue. The Demons have returned—stronger and more vicious than ever before. Your mission is clear, there are no options: Kill or be killed." "Doom" allows players to use more powerful and more gory weapons as the level of play progresses, so players can trade in shotguns for automatic weapons and then chain saws.

Another M-rated game, "Quake," has the following descriptions on the package, "Nail them to the wall," "Incorporates the ferocity of the single-player game with the supreme bloodlust of the two-player death match," and "Realistic explosions echo and reverberate, transporting the player to a hellish, dungeon-like environment." "Quake" sold more than 1.7 million copies the first year it was introduced. "Duke Nukem," rated M, advertises "32 levels of non-stop carnage" so the player can "Bag some aliens with over a dozen hi-tech weapons."

New video games with improved graphics and more realistic violence are constantly being developed. Video games also can be downloaded from the Internet and customized, adding a new dimension to the violence in keeping with individual preferences. Columbine killers Harris and Klebold customized "Doom" to graphically portray their neighborhood and school, allowing them to practice the shooting they would later enact in real life.

Does exposure to violence harm children?

What effect does exposure to this type of violence have on children? Studies of the effects of violent video games are limited, but investigations of the effects of violent television programming, which have been thoroughly evaluated during the past 50 years, offer insight.

In more than 1,000 studies, researchers have used laboratory-based exposure, population-based observations, and longitudinal analysis, among other methods, to document that children exposed to violent programming are more likely to behave in an aggressive or violent manner and are more likely to become involved with the justice system than children who have not had such exposure. Defenders of violent video games use the same argument as defenders of violent television do, however. They claim that the catharsis these games offer allows players to release aggressive tendencies.

To evaluate how violent video games affect children, one must consider the techniques these games rely on and what the literature shows about the games' impact. Unfortunately, most of the existing research was performed before 1993, the time after which violent content and realistic images began to increase greatly.

Exposure to violent video games is of even more concern than exposure to violence on television because the games take advantage of many of the principles of learning-identification (or participant modeling), practice and repetition, and reward and reinforcement.

Identification with the aggressor increases the likelihood that the participant will imitate behavior; in most violent video games, the player must identify with one violent character and perform violent acts through his eyes. The interactive nature of video games may also increase the likelihood that the participant will learn aggressive behavior. Adding to the increase in learning, the player of a video game is required to repeat behaviors. Last, video games reinforce violent choices with rewards of additional points, longer playing time, or special effects for certain acts of aggression or violence.

Parents are usually not aware of the nature of the video games their children are playing.

A recent study shows that physiologic changes associated with learning take place while playing video games. It demonstrated that striatal dopamine release increases during video game playing and that the correlation between dopamine release and performance level was significant. Dopaminergic neurotransmission is probably related to learning, reinforcement behavior, attention, and sensorimotor integration.

The profound effects of video games on learning

The profound effects of video games on learning were summed up by researchers J.B. Funk and D.D. Buchman, who wrote: "If, as many believe, violence is primarily a learned behavior, then the powerful combinations of demonstration, reward, and practice inherent in electronic game playing creates an ideal instructional environment. . . . the lessons being taught are that violence is fun, obligatory, easily justified, and essentially without negative consequences." The Columbine shooters are chilling examples of this principle. They were "Doom" fanatics who reconfigured a version of "Doom" to be in the "God mode" (the format in which the player becomes indestructible). The pair graphically reenacted the behavior they learned from the video game—they said the planned shooting was "going to be like f—ing 'Doom,'" "Tick, tick, tick, tick . . . Haa! That f—ing shotgun is straight out of 'Doom.'"

The type of learning that takes place may be influenced by the type of violent video game that is being played. Video games played on computers rely on the "mouse" to do the shootings, and players therefore learn strategies and warfare tactics. Video games played in arcades are much more likely to use "joysticks" or hand-operated devices that simulate pulling the trigger on the gun. Players of these games learn not only strategies but improve their hand-eye coordination and their aim. By joining "clans," online players can cooperate making battle plans and specialize in various aspects of warfare.

The most disconcerting and convincing argument for the hypothesis that violent video games teach violent behavior comes from Lieutenant Colonel David Grossman, a psychologist and adjunct professor at Arkansas State University, who specialized as a "killologist" for the United States military. After more than 25 years researching the psychology of killing for the Army, Grossman is convinced that the willingness to kill another person does not come naturally but is a learned behavior. It requires desensitization by repeated exposure to violence and classical conditioning by associating aggressive acts with a pleasant experience. Willingness to kill also relies on stimulus-response training so that the conditioned response (shooting a gun) becomes automatic with the right stimulus (alien or person in view).

Human violence is the main component of many video games.

According to Grossman, the United States Army and Marines use the same techniques that violent video games depend on to train recruits to kill. The Army also turns to an actual video game—"Doom"—to train soldiers to kill. This game, as well as "Quake" and similar games, teaches players to "clear the room" by moving quickly from target to target; to aim for the head; and to avoid repeatedly shooting the same target, as novices do. Grossman goes so far as to call violent video games "murder simulators."

People who have never fired a gun but have practiced shooting on video games are excellent marksmen when they fire a gun for the first time. A lawsuit filed against Michael Carneal, the 14-year-old Paducah, Kentucky boy who killed three students, alleges that Carneal "clipped off nine shots in about a 20-second period. Eight of those shots were hits. Three were head and neck shots and were kills. That is way beyond the military standard for expert marksmanship. This was a kid who had never fired a pistol in his life, but because of his obsession with computer games had turned himself into an expert marksman." According to Grossman, "Michael Carneal . . . fired eight shots . . . at a bunch of milling, scrambling, screaming children. . . . Even more astounding was the kill ratio. Each kid was hit once. Three were killed; one was paralyzed for life. Never, to my knowledge, in the annals of law enforcement or military or even criminal history can we find an equivalent achievement. . . . It turned out that while the kid had never fired a pistol before . . . he held the gun in two hands. He had a blank look on his face. He never moved his feet. He never fired too far to the right or the left or up or down. He simply fired one shot at everything that popped up on his screen."

What studies show

In 1997, the *Canadian Journal of Psychiatry* published a meta-analysis of 13 studies on the relationship between video games and aggression. Among the reviewed studies were some performed in the laboratory, where children played video games and were then observed during free play. One of those studies showed that 7- and 8-year-old boys who played video games with violent content were more likely to exhibit interpersonal aggression during free play than boys who had not played such games. In another study in the meta-analysis, researchers observed 5- to 7-year-old children after they played video games with aggressive or nonaggressive content and found that children who played a karate game were more likely to imitate the behavior seen in the game and were more aggressive than children who played a jungle game.

These studies have obvious limitations, including short duration of observation. The authors of the meta-analysis concluded, however, that "the majority of the studies show that children do become more aggressive after either playing or watching a violent video game."

Studies conducted in the 1980s that relied on questionnaires to correlate time spent playing video games and aggressive behavior provide conflicting results. Some studies demonstrated that playing video games increases aggressive behavior; others did not. In a study published in 2000, investigators surveyed college students about exposure to video game violence and self-reported aggressive behavior and delinquency. College students played a violent or nonviolent video game and then engaged in a competitive game in which they could punish their opponent by delivering a blast of noise, the length of which they could determine. Those who played violent games delivered significantly longer blasts after losing than nonviolent game players did. In a separate study outside the laboratory by the same investigators, violent video game play was positively related to aggressive behavior and delinquency.

Video games reinforce violent choices with rewards of additional points, longer playing time, or special effects for certain acts of aggression or violence.

A slightly earlier investigation found that third- and fourth-grade children who played a violent video game later provided more hostile interpretations of a story with an ambiguous ending (provocation story) than children who played a nonviolent game. Undergraduates who played a violent virtual reality game had more aggressive thoughts than students who simply observed the game.

According to a 1992 survey of sixth through 12th graders, playing violent video games contributed to an increase in aggressive behavior. Investigators also found that the longer a child played video games, the more likely she was to be considered aggressive by her teacher.

Correlational studies have also supported the relationship between violent video games and aggressive behavior. Interpol reported that, between 1977 and 1993, the assault rate in Australia and New Zealand increased almost 400%, tripled in Sweden, and doubled in Belgium, Denmark, England, France, and Scotland. Although these cultures differ in many ways, they have had a similar increase in violent video game exposure.

Some studies show no relationship between video game playing and aggression or violence. A 1987 study of eighth-grade students found that game play did not affect subsequent aggressive behavior. In another investigation, frequent users of video games seemed to play more when they were tense and felt more relaxed after playing.⌉

Findings in two studies performed in 1985 and in 1987 in 6- to 11-year-old children were conflicting. In the first study, children had more assertive fantasies after playing violent video games—a finding that the second study failed to confirm. Because these studies were conducted before the more violent and realistic video games were introduced, their results may not be applicable to today's environment.

More research into the long-term effects of video game playing is needed, especially in light of the recent improvements in the graphic display of games and the increase in their violent content.

Academic and educational concerns

Like watching television, playing video games displaces other activities of childhood, such as reading, playing outside, exercising or participating in sports, working on hobbies such as music or art activities, doing homework, or simply talking with friends and family. One study of 234 fourth-through sixth-grade students evaluated ratings of academic performance and various behaviors. A small but significant negative relationship was seen between arcade game use and teachers' ratings of math ability and general academic ability in boys. No such relationship was found when games were played at home. Another study that examined only "new game" use found that children were more likely to avoid homework when a new game was introduced, but over time played less frequently and for a shorter time.

Homework and chores were the activities most likely to be displaced by game playing, according to 21% of teens surveyed in a study from British Columbia. Teenagers who played video games more than seven hours a week were most likely to play games instead of participating in other activities; 37% of these heavy players said they played at the expense of homework and chores, and 18% said they gave up family activities. Research in this area is scanty, however, and results are often inconsistent.

⌈The Henry J. Kaiser Family Foundation, which has extensively studied children's use of all forms of media, found that children who earned lower academic grades spent about one hour more a day exposed to media than their counterparts with higher grades did. The study could not evaluate what caused the lower grades, and both groups of students spent about the same amount of time on video games. . . .⌉

What can be done?

Some data suggest that younger children are more at risk and that if children do not start playing video games until they reach adolescence, they are more likely to choose sport-oriented and strategic planning games (such as "SimCity") instead of first-person shooter games.

Encouraging parents to delay the introduction of video games may be an effective tool for decreasing children's exposure to violent games. Pediatricians also can encourage parents to be actively involved in their children's choice of media entertainment. . . . When a child has behavioral or academic problems, it is especially important to pay attention to how much time the child spends on interactive media. Parents should be aware that interventions to decrease television, video, and video game exposure have been shown to be effective. Third- and fourth-grade students in San Jose, Calif. who received a series of classroom lessons encouraging them to monitor and decrease their media use demonstrated less physical and verbal aggression when observed on the playground than students who didn't have the lessons. . . .

> *The United States Army and Marines use the same techniques that violent video games depend on to train recruits to kill.*

Parents who want to become advocates for wise video game choices in their community have several avenues. Recognizing that video game ratings are merely advisory, they can campaign local video stores, libraries, and arcades to require parental approval before a child can rent, buy, or play a video game with a T, M, or A rating. Another possibility is to conduct workshops and make presentations at schools and churches and in the community. Finally, consider contacting the manufacturers of violent video games and the Federal Communications Commission to urge them to limit violence in video games. Regardless of what intervention is chosen, the most important first step is to recognize that violent video games do indeed harm our children.

Notes

1. The Lion and Lamb Project aims to stop the marketing of violence to children. The organization's "Dirty Dozen" list contains an annual list of violence-oriented toys and games parents should avoid.

2. Titles rated "Mature (M)" are suited for persons 17 and over. May include strong language and violence and mature sexual themes. Titles rated "Teen (T)" are suited for ages 13 and over and may contain violence and mildly graphic language. "Adult (A)" rated titles are for adults only and contain content not suited for minors.

2

The Problem of Video Game Violence Is Exaggerated

Greg Costikyan

Greg Costikyan is a game designer currently with Unplugged Games. He also writes frequently about gaming and is the author of four novels.

Violence has become commonplace in video games and is often portrayed in a graphic, grisly fashion. However, violence is only part of the whole aesthetic in most games. Violent first-person shooter games are not simply virtual shooting sprees—they also engage players in exploration and puzzle solving. Furthermore, first-person shooter games actually benefit society because they allow players to express their violent impulses in ways that are not antisocial. The current attack on video games echoes the irrational fears that fueled the hysteria surrounding comic books, pinball machines, and other benign youth culture phenomena.

About 10 years ago, I had drinks with Frank Chadwick, then president of a game publisher called Game Designers Workshop. At the time, the Game Manufacturers Association was trying to reposition hobby games as "adventure games"—which we both thought risible.

Chadwick said, "You know, a better name for our industry would be 'violence gaming.'"

I flinched, of course. But Chadwick had a point: hobby games then consisted mainly of war games—war is certainly violent—and role-playing games, whose players spend much of their time in combat against fantastic monsters or comic-book supervillains and such.

Violence is intrinsic to many, many games. Even as abstract a game as chess can be seen as a form of military conflict.

When I was a kid, "gaming" meant the mass-market boardgame industry and a small hobby-game appendage that together grossed perhaps a few hundred million dollars at retail. Today, it includes computer, console and arcade gaming and is a $7 billion industry in the U.S. alone—the second largest entertainment industry in the world, after film and television.

As [author] Marshall McLuhan would have it, every medium has a message. If violence is intrinsic to gaming, and if gaming is an increasingly predominant form of entertainment, is the likely consequence to our society an increase in violence?

Are the critics who attack gaming in the wake of the Littleton massacre[1] correct on the fundamentals? Should Congress ask the surgeon general to prepare a report on how video games spur youth violence, as it is considering? Do games stoke our violent instincts—or sublimate them? Is there such a thing as "good violence" and "bad violence" in games? Let's step back a moment. What *is* a game?

What is a game?

A game is an interactive structure that requires players to struggle toward a goal.

If there's no interaction, it isn't a game; it's a puzzle. If there's no goal, then the players have no reason to choose one option over another, to undertake one task instead of something else; there's no structure. If achieving the goal isn't a struggle, if winning is easy, the game is dull; winning's no thrill.

Struggle implies conflict. Just as conflict is at the core of every story, conflict is at the core of every game. That doesn't mean all conflict must be violent; in a story, the central conflict can be the protagonist's own feelings of inadequacy, or the obduracy of her in-laws, or the inequities of society. But violent conflict has its uses; otherwise, we wouldn't have horror stories and mysteries and thrillers. Not to mention *Hamlet* and *Henry V*.

There are as many ways to create conflict in a game as in a story. Adventure games like Myst use puzzles. Games like Diplomacy require negotiation. Builder games like Civilization require you to overcome economic and technological obstacles.

But there's no way to avoid conflict entirely. No conflict, no struggle. No struggle, no obstacles. No obstacles, no work. No work, no fun

Where does violence come into the picture? Violence is an easy out. It's the simplest, most obvious way to make a game a struggle. If achieving your goal requires you to get through a horde of ravenous, flesh-eating monsters, the conflict is clear—and the way to win is equally clear. You kill them.

Games are not about violence. Games are about struggle.

Obstacles-of-violence, to coin a term, are compelling; the kill-or-be-killed instinct is wired into our hind-brain, part of our vertebrate heritage. Games like Quake II trigger a visceral, edge-of-the-seat response. Precisely because you can be killed at any moment by strange and nasty creatures, because only quick reactions can defeat them, Quake is a compelling experience.

Quake uses violence well. By that, I mean that it achieves precisely the effect its designers wished to achieve, and succeeds in delivering a compelling, stimulating, entertaining, intense experience to the player. It is a fine game.

But still: Violence is not the *only* way to achieve struggle in games. It is merely the easiest, the simplest, the most obvious tool in the game designer's armamentarium.

So—are games fundamentally violent and therefore bad? No. Chadwick was wrong; games are not *about* violence. Games are about struggle. Because violence is the easiest way to create struggle, many games are violent—but far from all.

But perhaps a more sophisticated argument still holds water? Perhaps game designers have insouciantly awoken the beast, cavalierly creating entertainment so violently compelling that it teaches violence, desensitizes us, spurs increased violence in our society?

Violence is, and should be, part of a designer's toolkit; but it is neither necessary nor sufficient.

There *is* a lot of violence in computer gaming. Some of it is very ugly. The two most popular categories in computer games at present are the first-person shooter (Quake, Unreal, Half-Life) and the real-time strategy game (StarCraft, Myth, Total Annihilation). Both categories are "games of violence," if you will.

The computer gaming industry is a monoculture: It consists almost entirely of white, suburban males in their 20s. We're talking the demographic that reads *Maxim* magazine. They're heavily into computer games, almost completely ignorant of games from other media and almost equally ignorant of computer games published longer than five years ago. Visiting a game development firm is like walking into a strangely 1950s version of 1990s America; if any women are on the premises, they're artists or marketing people. You may see some Asians, you might see a programmer from India, but certainly nobody darker.

Arresting images

Developers play the same games, they see the same movies, they fraternize with people like themselves and they develop some pretty weird mind-sets. Violence is perceived as cool—no, not real violence, but violence in games.

Consider Postal, published two years ago. It's a shooter in which you play a deranged, psychotic loser. You wander around shooting completely innocent people at random.

It's hard to imagine why anyone thought this was a good idea. For one thing, innocent people do not make good obstacles: They're unlikely to shoot back. They're not particularly threatening. Never mind the moral considerations; this makes for a dull game.

And the moral considerations should certainly have made Postal's developers (a company called Running With Scissors) think twice. No doubt, they assumed that the "edgy" nature of the project would get them a lot of press and boost its sales. They did get a lot of press, almost all of it negative, and no doubt that did spur some sales to the kind of people who actually think "Beavis & Butthead" is funny.

But you know what? Postal failed. It didn't achieve anywhere near expected sales. The reviews were almost uniformly negative. It failed because it was a bad game.

Consider the "bathtub of blood" ad (for the game Blood, developed by Monolith for GT Interactive). It ran in computer gaming magazines in 1997 (for example, the front gatefold of *Computer Gaming World,* May 97). The dominant image of the advertisement was, literally, a bathtub filled with blood.

It's hard to imagine why *anyone* thought this was effective advertising. What it said was: Our game is violent. Our sense of humor is crass. It didn't actually do what an advertisement *must* do—explain why the product will be fun or useful, establish a compelling value proposition for the consumer.

Only computer game developers could ever have thought this was a good idea.

In March 1999, another advertisement, for an online games retailer, appeared in the computer gaming press (for instance, *Computer Gaming World,* March 99, page 89). Its dominant image is that of the naked torso of a woman, lying on an operating table, the rest of her body outside the frame. In the foreground are surgically-gloved hands, holding a scalpel. In the woman's bare flesh are incised the lines of a tic-tac-toe game.

I buy a lot of computer games. I generally buy them online. But the image of someone cutting a woman's flesh in order to play the most patently brain-dead game imaginable did not make me want to patronize this company's services. God only knows why they thought it would motivate anyone else.

Certainly, it is an arresting image. Arresting enough to make the gorge rise. Only the computer gaming culture could possibly view any of this as effective, appropriate or funny.

So perhaps the critics are correct, at least to this degree: The coolness of violence, as portrayed in computer games, has persuaded computer game developers, if no one else, that nauseating depictions of violence, whether or not effective, are cool.

In the gaming field, the response to post-Littleton attacks has been self-righteously defensive. It's just a game. It doesn't hurt you any more than TV (never mind the damage television has done to our political system, our propensity to read, and our sense of social solidarity). Games Are Cool.

That's understandable. Computer gaming people have virtually no defense *other* than self-righteousness. They're guilty of many of the sins ascribed to them.

But consider this: The excesses fail. Postal failed. Those ads do not deliver. Violence alone doesn't do the trick. Violence is, and should be, part of a designer's toolkit; but it is neither necessary nor sufficient.

The artistic use of violence

Every year, Brian Moriarty gives a speech at the Game Developers Conference, one of the industry's main trade shows. Every year, it is the best-received speech at the conference. Moriarty is a brilliant speaker, but more than that, he is one of the industry's *eminences grises*—one of the original Infocom crew, creator of Loom and Beyond Zork, now in charge of development at MPlayer (one of the biggest of the online-game communities).

Last year, Moriarty's speech was on the subject of violence in games. As he spoke, two short clips appeared on a screen behind him, repeating hypnotically. One was a clip from "The Great Train Robbery," a silent film historians call the first real movie hit, showing a mustachioed Westerner shooting a gun directly toward the camera; the other, a short sequence from Quake, showed a guard being shot.

Compelling images both—and compelling in that both show that violence has been an important part of two very different media, virtually from their inceptions.

The speech itself was a meditation on two issues: first, the nature of violence in gaming; and second, the idea of "rhythm of play." Moriarty says that, if you observe people playing a game—observe them, not the game itself—you find that they engage in repeated cycles of activity. And this repetition, the rhythm created, is one of the strongest draws for people to interactive entertainment. It's hypnotic. It's involving.

Violence used artistically is effective; violence used crudely is vile.

Violence, he says, creates dissonance. It breaks the rhythm. Dissonance is not bad in itself; dissonance, consciously and creatively used, can be an extremely effective technique, in gaming as in music.

"If you want to include violence in your games," says Moriarty, "do it, and put your heart and soul into it, do it with awareness—not because violence is easy, or because it shocks, but because you need dissonance, and you know how and why it strengthens your game."

To paraphrase: Violence used artistically is effective; violence used crudely is vile.

It's a lesson most computer-game developers have yet to learn—and if one of the upshots of Littleton is that they begin to think more clearly about the issue, that will be to the good.

Training for murder?

First-person shooters are violent games. Yet they are not depictions of endless, orgasmic mayhem; in their solo-play mode, they are mainly about exploration and puzzle-solving, with opposition provided in the form of monsters you shoot. Though violence, and the edge-of-the-seat tension it builds, is a key part of the game's aesthetic, impressive 3D technology and art and clever "level design" (where exploration and puzzle-solving come in) are at least as important.

The "violence" is against monsters, defined as such, who are clearly attempting to kill you; the back story, such as it is, presents them as some kind of horrible, Lovecraftian intrusion into the real world. Hence they are, in a sense, totally depersonalized opponents. But the notion that this kind of thing therefore "desensitizes" people to violence and makes them more willing to commit it seems dubious. Shooters are really about the "booga-booga" fright instinct: A scary monster appears out of nowhere and roars at you; you have to turn quickly and blow it away.

And of course, you die frequently yourself. The feeling engendered is not "I'm an immortal Rambo, I'm so cool I can kill anything"—rather, it's more like, "God, that was a hard level, those spider things with the cannon launchers are really tough, I'm glad I finally got through it."

Interestingly, the multiplayer online version is very different. You shoot not monsters but other players, who are running around trying to kill you. And they aren't depersonalized; they look just like you, you can chat with them (but rarely do because the game is too fast-paced), and so forth. This has been portrayed as something new and frightening—but frankly, it's no different from paintball and not much different from tag.

The press has reported Lt. Col. David Grossman's claim that games like Quake are good training for murder, because they teach you to "clear a room" by moving quickly from target to target and aiming for the head. They teach you to avoid the novice hunter or soldier's mistake of shooting repeatedly at the same target until the target drops, and instead to use only a single shot.

On the basis of this, I have to doubt that Grossman has ever actually played Quake. No monster in Quake can be killed with a single shot; at least two hits are required. It is impossible to make a "head-shot"; Quake makes no distinction between shots that strike at different locations on a target's body. And if you stay still long enough to pick your targets and get off head-shots, you're dead. You must keep moving to evade enemy fire. You snap off shots when you can.

The development of shooting games over time has not been toward more and more megaviolence.

In short, Quake doesn't teach the lessons that the critics claim it teaches. The development of shooting games over time has not been toward more and more megaviolence; rather, it's been toward prettier and more-impressive 3D rendering (Unreal) and toward more compelling story-lines, interwoven more effectively with the game (Half-Life).

Yes, these are violent games—but as is usually the case when the media latches onto something, they have been caricatured. Violence is only a part of their appeal.

Immutable violent impulses

The idea that film or television or books make people violent has been debunked again and again. (For one thing, if it were true, Japan would, judging by its popular culture, surely be filled with violent pederasts instead of the civilized world's most peaceful and orderly population.)

But perhaps computer games are different—so uniquely compelling that violence in games does breed violent behavior?

Some 25 years ago, I read through the *Whole Earth Catalog*. One section of the book was devoted to the war games published by Simulations Publications Inc.—and I was then an avid war gamer (and later employed by that company) so I, naturally, read it carefully. *The Whole Earth Catalog* was written during the Vietnam War, a period when schools shied away from any discussion of warfare or military history as too hot a topic to consider. But, as the publication said, war has been part of human nature since time immemorial. War is worthy of study, if only so that we can avoid it by understanding it more fully. And, perhaps, war games are our best hope of avoiding future wars. Perhaps the things we find attractive about war, perhaps the impulses that lead us to war, can be satisfied through simulation.

Violent computer games channel antisocial impulses in societally acceptable ways.

Violence, and the attraction of violence, is a fundamental part of human nature. It is particularly appealing to young adolescent males, for it is a clean break with the rules-bound environment in which they have lived, a rejection of parental order. In every society, violence is most common among young men.

It is foolish to try to change human nature; it is immutable, or mutable only through the slow process of evolution. What can be changed is society. Society can develop institutions and mechanisms to channel antisocial impulses to pro-social purposes. That's one reason for armies, of course; they institutionalize violence in a mechanism designed to protect rather than damage society.

And games of violence? They allow players to *be* violent, to act out their violent impulses, to hunt and shoot and kill—in a way that harms no one.

Listen to the boastfulness of Quake players on TEN. They'll kill your pussy ass. They'll blow you up so good your spleen will land in Chicago and your liver in Des Moines. They're profane and obnoxious, and violently so.

They're blowing up pixels. They're killing bitmaps. They're shooting at software subroutines.

They're not a threat to public order, for chrissakes. What they're doing makes them less likely to be a threat to public order. They're getting their jones—they're satisfying their antisocial impulses in a completely harmless way.

Violent computer games don't spur violence; violent computer games channel antisocial impulses in societally acceptable ways.

Games are good.

Gaming déjà vu

For those of us who've been involved in gaming for a long time, the whole hysteria over Littleton brings forth a strong sense of *déjà vu*.

We've been through this before. Fifteen years ago, Dungeons & Dragons was the culprit. Every time some kid killed himself and a copy of

D&D was found amid the stuff in his room, the papers would run a story about how those vile fantasy role-playing games made him do it. The fundamentalists latched onto it, too; Dungeons & Dragons involved magic and spells, and to fundamentalists of a certain stripe, that means it must be inherently demonic and evil.

Poor Sandy Petersen is the man I sympathized with most. He designed Call of Cthulhu, a role-playing game based on the horror stories of H.P. Lovecraft. He's a devout Mormon. His game was repeatedly attacked, and he along with it, as one of the most demonic and evil of the lot: After all, it deals explicitly with demons from other dimensions. He found himself on panels at gaming conventions, trying to explain to gamers that all Christians were not vile, censoring, irrational scum—and I have no doubt he found himself trying to explain to his co-religionists why all gamers weren't evil Satanic monsters.

If I feel a sense of déjà vu, how much worse it must be for him. Sandy co-designed Doom II and Quake.

It's not just Dungeons & Dragons. We went through this when the Internet first came to prominence, and was blamed for sex crimes and pederasty. We went through it in the '50s, when comic books were attacked as perverting our youth, leading to the death of EC Comics and the establishment of the Comics Code Authority. We went through it in the '30s, when LaGuardia took his hatchet to pinball machines across New York.

Hell, we went through it with rock 'n' roll.

Young people are the ones most open to novelty. Consequently, they lead the way in the adoption of any new entertainment medium. Parent/teenager relationships being what they are, parents invariably view the new medium as threatening. The nature of our journalism-industrial complex being what it is, some pundits seize on the fear as a means of achieving an audience. The most threatening aspects of the medium are puffed up into a major threat to civilization. Kids find their medium under attack, and respond, naturally, by embracing the aspects under attack most wholeheartedly.

Sometimes, as with Dungeons & Dragons, the attack ultimately dissipates under the weight of its own ludicrous contradictions. Sometimes, as with EC Comics, congressional hearings and an abject surrender by the industry result.

But these attacks, all of them, have nothing to do with reality. They're about fear. They're about the fear of the new—the fear of parents who see their children doing something they don't understand and worry about the consequences.

Argument from ignorance

The attack is an argument from ignorance. It has no rational basis. It is made by people who don't understand what they attack, and find its indicia frightening. And to the degree that they have any credibility at all, it's because ugly and repulsive violence *does* exist within computer gaming. And if the industry has the brains God gave a biscuit, it will respond—not by imposing censorship or another inane rating scheme, but by avoiding the kind of repulsive, exploitative violence that any idiot ought to see is not going to work anyway.

If *you* are concerned about violence in gaming, I have one piece of advice: Go buy a copy of Quake II. Install it on your machine. Download a walkthrough, so you won't fear humiliation when you play. And give it a try.

I think you'll find that it's not so frightening. You may even have a good time.

You might even find yourself—like me—shopping for a home networking kit and running cable, so you can play games with your kids.

Note

1. On April 20, 1999, at Columbine High School in Littleton, Colorado, two student gunmen killed twelve students and a teacher before turning the guns on themselves.

3

Video Games Rated Appropriate for Children May Contain Violence

Kimberly M. Thompson and Kevin Haninger

Kimberly M. Thompson is assistant professor of Risk Analysis and Decision Science at the Harvard School of Public Health at Harvard University. Kevin Haninger is a doctoral student in health policy at the same university.

In 1994 the Interactive Digital Software Association (IDSA), a U.S. association that serves business and public affairs needs, voluntarily created the Entertainment Software Rating Board (ESRB) to review and rate the contents of all video games. Their rating and content descriptions, which are placed on game packaging and in advertisements, suggest which games are appropriate for players of all ages or suitable only for teenagers or adults. Games are rated on the basis of the use of strong language, graphic depiction of violent acts, and presence of adult themes such as sexuality and drug and alcohol use. The ESRB's implementation of a game rating system has been lauded, but a closer look reveals that many games rated "E" for Everyone actually contain acts of violence in which video game characters are intentionally injured or killed. Consequently, parents should take an active role in assessing the content of E-rated games before permitting their children to play them.

Created in 1994, the Entertainment Software Rating Board (ESRB) rates video games according to categories listed in the Box and using content descriptors, which game manufacturers display on the game box to inform consumer choices. Analogous to the G rating of films, the E rating (for "Everyone") of video games suggests suitability for all audiences, but the E rating does not mean violence-free.

Studies on children's use of various media document the popularity of video games as a major source of entertainment. A recent study found that 70% of children (age, 2–18 years) live in homes that have at least 1 video game console, 33% of children have video game consoles in their bedrooms, and 30% of children in the study played video games the previous day. Children in the study reported playing video games for 20 min/d on average, although older children (age, 8–18 years) accounted for most of this use (average, 27 min/d), with boys spending significantly more time playing video games than girls and white children playing video games for significantly less time than black or Hispanic children. Unfortunately, little information exists about the ratings and genres of the games that children play as a function of their age, sex, family income level, and ethnicity, although some differences in preferences exist. Overall, children appear to play relatively more games in the action, adventure, and sports genres, but this may simply reflect the types of games available.

The health implications of exposure to video games and other media with violent content remain uncertain, but considerable concern about the potential impacts of children experiencing media violence exists within the broad medical community. Although several recent studies repeat concerns about the content of video games and the marketing of violent entertainment to children, more research on the impact of violent interactive entertainment, including video games, is needed. Remarkably, no quantitative analysis exists on content in E-rated video games or on the relationship between game content and the ESRB content descriptors. This study focuses on providing quantitative information to physicians and parents about the content of E-rated video games.

Methods

Video game console systems continue to evolve with 3 manufacturers presently dominating the market: Nintendo, maker of Nintendo 64 (N64); Sony, maker of PlayStation (PS) and PlayStation 2 (PS2); and Sega, maker of Dreamcast (DC). Popular arcade games featuring different types of game play (eg, Space Invaders, Pole Position, Donkey Kong) served as the first home video games and gave rise to the modern video game market with its wide variety of games of different genres. We created a database of information about the universe of E-rated games available for rent or sale in the United States by April 1, 2001 (accessible at http://www. kidsrisk.harvard.edu) because we expected that the level of violence in video games might depend on genre. The process involved using data from the ESRB and several Internet sites to identify all 672 E-rated console games, verify that each game was released in the United States, determine each game's content descriptor(s), and classify each game by 1 of 11 primary genres: action, adventure, casino, fighting, puzzle, racing, role-playing, shooting, simulation, sports, and strategy. A small number of games could not be classified by these genres and were labeled as other. Unfortunately, the subjective process of characterizing game play, as well as the complexity introduced by the growing presence of games of hybrid genres, have prevented a universal system for classifying video games by genre. For example, one of the most popular games in our sample, The Legend of Zelda: Ocarina of Time, is classified as action, adventure, or role-playing on different Internet sites. In such cases, we selected the genre that was most commonly used to describe the game. Using the database, we then performed statistical analyses to summarize the distribution of games by genre and content descriptors.

To quantitatively assess the content of games, we selected 55 E-rated video games that represented the distribution of content descriptors and genres and that were available for play on one of the current major home video game consoles in the United States (DC, N64, PS, or PS2). We designed the study to include several games on each console and to play a mixture of both the highly popular games as well as ones that did not receive widespread consumer interest.

Considerable concern about the potential impacts of children experiencing media violence exists within the broad medical community.

To explore the possibility of trends in series of video games, we also selected 2 of the most popular series by sales for study: The Legend of Zelda series in the adventure genre and the Super Mario Bros. series in the action genre. We played all of the games in these series, including games released for older consoles like Nintendo Entertainment System and Super Nintendo Entertainment System. Since the 2 oldest games in The Legend of Zelda series were released prior to the creation of the ESRB and have not been rated, we did not include them in our analysis of E-rated games even though we are confident that these games would receive E ratings. Finally, for historical comparison, we assessed the content of 8 classic arcade games that have been rereleased as E-rated compilations or paired with E-rated remakes of the original games. Overall, we played a total of 65 games.

For consistency, an undergraduate student with considerable video gaming experience played all of the games and recorded all game play directly onto videocassettes for later coding. The student played each game to its conclusion or for at least 90 minutes, whichever occurred first. Some action and adventure games that allow the player to save game progress are designed for very long play times; consequently, not playing these games to their conclusion means that some content is missed. In particular, some games may become more difficult as the player advances and they may offer additional weapons or other more mature content. However, in our effort to strike a reasonable balance between playing more games and playing individual games for longer times, we determined that playing the game to its conclusion or for at least 90 minutes allowed us to obtain a reasonably good sample of game play for any single game. Video games often start with an introduction and setup, which the player may elect to bypass. Consequently, we did not include introductions and game setup in our coding or calculations of the duration of game play, although we did generally observe them. For consistency, we defined the beginning of game play as the first scene where autonomous movement occurred.

With the game play recorded on videocassettes for consistency, one author, who also has considerable video gaming experience, reviewed and coded all of the games using a standard coding instrument and entered the data into a database. . . . The first author and the game player each independently coded a subset of 10 games to assess intercoder reliability. We discussed all instances of games that presented difficulty in coding with verification of game details from the undergraduate student who played the games. We performed descriptive and statistical analyses . . . to compare our sample to the universe of E-rated games.

We defined violence as acts in which the aggressor causes or attempts to cause physical injury or death to another character. We did not include accidental actions that led to unintentional physical harm, the effects of natural disasters, or the presence of dangerous obstacles that could not be attributed to the actions of a particular character. A violent incident was defined as an uninterrupted display of violence by a character or a group of characters. We defined characters broadly, including personified objects that attacked either the player or other characters. We did not code as violence any intentional acts of physical force that represent normal play in a sports game (eg, tackling in football or checking in hockey), because the intention of the player is technically to stop the other player without causing injury. We did code excessive physical contact in sports games, such as punching or otherwise attacking another player (eg, after the football play was over). To quantify the amount of violence, we manually recorded the starting and ending times of each incident of violence toward other characters (hours, minutes, and seconds from the beginning of the tape).

In the sample of 55 games played, 27 games (49%) depicted deaths from violence.

In video games, characters often engage in a series of violent acts that are punctuated by brief periods of time spent running toward the next encounter. For consistency, we established a rule that a series of violent acts would be coded as 1 violent incident only if individual acts of violence were separated by fewer than 10 seconds of nonviolent behavior. For each violent incident, we recorded the type of weapons used for violence, whether the violent incident resulted in injury, and the number of character deaths attributable to the violent incident. In addition, for each game, we noted whether injuring characters or destroying objects is rewarded or is necessary to advance in the game, whether the player could select weapons, and whether any of the following content was present: alcohol, tobacco, illegal drugs, profanity, and sex. Finally, we also looked for the presence of music from explicit-content-labeled recordings, because a recent Federal Trade Commission report found that 2 music companies had approved the use of music with parental advisory labels in E-rated video games.

Analysis of E-rated video games

Our analysis of the universe of E-rated video games led to a database of 672 games with 99% of these games available for play on at least 1 of the major home consoles in our study (DC, N64, PS, or PS2). Of these 672 games, our sample included 55 games (8.2%). Half (28 of 55 games) appeared on the monthly list that ranks the 25 best-selling games in the

United States by units sold (regardless of ratings). In the context of coding, we found good agreement between the author who coded all of the games and the student who played them. . . .

Based on analysis of the 672 E-rated video games released for home consoles, games in the sports (28%), racing (26%), and action (23%) genres account for most of the games. Again, our sample has a similar distribution to the universe of E-rated games, although our effort to explore trends in 2 series of video games contributed to our over-sampling of games from the action and adventure genres. . . .

No games provide messages about not using violence.

In our sample of 55 games played, we found 20 games that did not include violent game play, and 35 games (64%) that involved intentional violence, with an average of 30.7% of the game duration representing violent game play for these games (range, 1.5%–91.2%). We found that injuring characters was rewarded or required for advancement in 33 (60%) games. Separating the 55 games into 2 groups, 1 group containing 23 games that received a content descriptor for violence and 1 group containing 32 games that did not receive a content descriptor for violence, we found that the games with a violence descriptor contained significantly more violence. . . . Remarkably, we also found that 14 of the 32 games (44%) that received no content descriptors contained acts of violence an average of 37% of the game duration. All of the games we played in the action, adventure, fighting, shooting, strategy, and simulation genres included violence, while only 2 of the sports games (17%) included violence not associated with normal game play. Given the relatively small sample size, however, we caution against overgeneralization of these particular results.

In the sample of 55 games played, 27 games (49%) depicted deaths from violence. Not surprisingly, the shooting game showed the highest numbers of deaths per minute (23.8). In all 22 of the action games, we found that injuring characters was rewarded or was required to advance in the game. Nearly all of the action games (21/22 [95%]) depicted deaths from violence, with an average (arithmetic mean) of 2.3 deaths per minute (range, 0 deaths per minute for Paperboy to 8.4 deaths per minute for Rat Attack).

We observed that each successive game within The Legend of Zelda series had progressively less violence and fewer deaths per minute; a less clear trend was demonstrated for the Super Mario Bros. series. One explanation that is consistent with our experience is that successive games in series may tend to involve more complexity in character development and engage the player in more exploration and discovery activities that will help him/her achieve a goal. However, this trend of less violence may be offset by the tendency for successive games to portray violence more graphically and more realistically as technology advances. The limited evidence of these 2 series should not be overgeneralized.

Although damage to objects was not coded as violence in our analysis, we found that games rewarded characters for destroying objects or re-

quired object destruction for advancement in 29 of 55 games (53%). A total of 30 of 55 games (55%) used the body as a weapon, 27 games (49%)
used projectiles, 16 games (29%) used magic, 13 games (24%) used guns,
6 games (11%) used a knife or sword, 2 games (4%) used toxic substances
(poisons), 17 games (33%) used explosives, and 26 games (47%) used
other weapons (eg, fire, hammers, snowboard). This is not an exhaustive
list of the weapons that might be encountered in the games because of
the limited amount of time that each game was played; consequently, it
should be viewed as a subset of the weapons depicted in these games.

In addition to coding for violence, we also noted other content in the
games that might have led the ESRB to assign content descriptors to the
game. For example, Goemon's Great Adventure and NFL Blitz 2000 received ESRB content descriptors for "mild language." We found the word
"damn" printed on the screen in Goemon's Great Adventure and noted
that the players taunt each other in NFL Blitz 2000. Although none of the
games received a content descriptor for "suggestive themes," we noted
the provocative leather outfit worn by Ai Fukami in Ridge Racer V, the
screen shot between her thighs, and the phrases "Control your desire"
and "push it to the limit" in the introduction. We also noted sexual in-
nuendo in Gex 3: Deep Cover Gecko. Finally, in Harvest Moon 64, which
received a content rating "use of tobacco and alcohol," the player can
choose to purchase and consume beer, wine, or liquor resulting in a red
face and a fall to the floor. We did not find any depiction of tobacco in
our play of that game or find any music with parental advisories in any
of the games played in our sample.

Considerable variability of E-rated games

The first public outcry over violence in video games occurred in 1976,
when Exidy Games withdrew from the market Death Race 2000, a game
that awarded players points for running over stick figures. In the 1980s, the
US government began using video games for military training purposes,
and recently [retired Army Ranger] Dave Grossman and [media violence ex-
pert] Gloria DeGaetano publicized the use of off-the-shelf video games in
military battle training. Controversy and concern about the effects of video
games on children continue, although much remains to be learned.

---

*In [the E-rated game] Harvest Moon 64 . . . the player
can choose to purchase and consume beer, wine, or
liquor resulting in a red face and a fall to the floor.*

With all of the questions about the impact of violence in video games
on children, this is the first study to our knowledge to quantify the
amount of violence in E-rated video games and to show that many E-rated
games do involve violence, killing, and the use of weapons in the course
of normal play. No games provide messages about not using violence, and
some games reward or require violence and the destruction of objects.

The video game genre, ESRB rating, and ESRB content descriptors provide important information about the content of the game, and overall

illustrate the considerable variability that exists in the universe of E-rated games. One implication of this finding is that studies that assess video game content with a mix of games of different ratings and genres might produce very different results than studies that focus on a single rating and genre; future researchers will need to carefully consider the process of selecting the games for their samples. Clearly, efforts to standardize definitions for genres would be both challenging and helpful.

Many E-[rated] games contain a significant amount of violence and demonstrate ambiguity in what constitutes [the description of] "minimal violence."

The content descriptors appear to provide limited information about violence. We found that receiving any content descriptor for violence (animated violence, mild animated violence, etc) provided a good indication of violence in the game, but the absence of a descriptor did not mean violence-free. The definition for the E rating states that the game "may contain minimal violence," yet our experience shows that many E-games contain a significant amount of violence and demonstrate ambiguity in what constitutes "minimal violence." We did not see how the ESRB distinguishes between different content descriptors for violence and we believe that efforts to standardize the definitions of content descriptors would be helpful. Another approach to consider would be to have content descriptors that provide information about the amount of violence using a scale instead of noting simply its presence. This might help consumers distinguish among games that receive the same descriptors but contain very different amounts of violence (eg, Nuclear Strike 64 vs 40 Winks or Rat Attack vs The Smurfs). We also noted some inconsistencies between games that received a content descriptor and games that did not.

Currently, the ESRB rates games based on information and materials submitted by the game manufacturer, but does not play the game before assigning the rating. While giving the same materials to raters may promote consistency, our experience playing the games leads us to believe that the ESRB raters should play the finished game, including the introduction, before assigning a rating.

Remarkably, we found some nearly identical games that received different ratings on different consoles (eg, Nuclear Strike 64 and Gex 3: Deep Cover Gecko are E-rated on N64 but rated T for "Teen" on PS), which may make game selection more confusing. We believe that the ESRB should avoid assigning different ratings of the same game on different platforms and should assign the highest rating to all of the games of the same title to avoid inadvertently misleading consumers who may not appreciate the differences between platforms.

A few important limitations exist in this study. First, the sample of games represents only a small subset of the available E-rated games. Second, the results depend on the actual game play that we recorded and the methods we used for coding information, which include subjective judgment in the definitions and their implementation. . . .

Third, our use of a broad definition of violence focused on the intention of the character may differ from other similarly legitimate definitions. For example, the sports and racing games, essentially all of which receive an E rating, provided the greatest challenges to coding because they contain intended acts of physical contact like checking in hockey and tackling in football that are not intended to cause injury, although other studies or coders might deem these acts to be "violent."

Despite these limitations, this study provides important and useful information to physicians and parents about the content of E-rated games. Parents should be aware of games' ratings, content descriptors, and genres, and parents whose children play games should actively participate in game selection and engage their children in discussion of the game content. Several Internet sites also provide helpful information for parents who want to better understand the content of video games. In addition to the ESRB Web site, the National Institute on Media and the Family's KidScore media evaluation system offers information to parents about many types of content in video games. . . .

Our content analysis suggests that many E-rated video games contain a significant amount of violence and that an "E" rating does not automatically signify a level of violence acceptable for very young game players. Physicians and parents should understand that popular E-rated video games may be a source of exposure to violence for children that rewards them for violent actions and that they may contain other content that is not expected given the E rating. We believe that physicians, particularly pediatricians, should consider asking patients about their experience with video games and the medical and public health communities should play an active role in informing parents about the content in video games.

4

The Video Game Industry Regulates Itself Effectively

Douglas Lowenstein

Douglas Lowenstein is president of the Interactive Digital Software Association (IDSA), an organization that serves the business and public affairs needs of entertainment software companies. IDSA accounts for the majority of entertainment software sold in the United States.

The Interactive Digital Software Association (IDSA) responsibly regulates the content of entertainment software in the United States. In 1994, the IDSA established the Entertainment Software Rating Board (ESRB) to review and rate every video game. The ESRB suggests the age appropriateness of games based on the amount of graphic violence, strong language, or provocative themes they contain. The board has also initiated many nationwide programs to increase consumer and retailer awareness of the rating system. As a result, research has shown that adults believe that the ESRB's ratings are reliable and effective, helping them choose which games are suitable for their children.

First, let me address two of the great myths about the video game industry, to wit: 1) video games are played predominantly by teenage boys and 2) most video games are rated Mature and have significant levels of violence. Both are wrong.

The primary audience

In fact, the primary audience for video games is NOT adolescent boys. According to research by Peter D. Hart Research Associates in 2000, the average age of computer and video game players is 28 years old, and 61 percent of all game players are age 18 and over. A remarkable 35% of game players are over 35 years old, and 13% are over 50; 43% of the 145 million Americans who play computer and video games are women. Interactive Digital Software Association's (IDSA) own consumer research reveals that 70% of the most frequent users of computer games and 57% of the

Excerpted from Douglas Lowenstein's testimony before the Senate Committee on Commerce, September 13, 2000.

most frequent users of video games are also over 18.

Unlike other entertainment products, most newly released video games cost anywhere from $40–60. Thus, it's not surprising, when you add this to the fact that a majority of consumers are adults, that IDSA research finds that nine out of every ten video games are actually purchased by someone over 18. Furthermore, 84% of the kids who do buy games say they have the permission of their parents to do so. Similarly, in a survey completed by [researcher] Peter Hart in the fall of 1999, 83% of parents said they "try to watch or play at least once every game that their child plays to determine whether it is appropriate."

Notably, the Federal Trade Commission's (FTC) own survey confirms these findings. "It is clear that most parents are able to play a watchdog role when they choose to do so. . . . According to parents' responses, even more parents (83%) are involved in the actual purchase transaction; 38% report that they usually purchase or rent the games, and another 45% of parents do so together with the child."

Contrary to popular perceptions, most [video] games do not contain significant levels of violence.

So any discussion of how our industry markets its products must take into account the fact that a majority of those who buy and use our products are adults, not kids, so parents are still almost certainly going to be involved in the actual purchase. As the FTC said, "This level of parental involvement, either at the point of selection or purchase, means that most parents have the opportunity to review rating information or to check the product packaging to determine whether they approve of the game's content."

This does not mean our industry does not have an obligation to market products responsibly and to label them accurately. But it does mean that parents are the first, last, and best line of defense against products that are not appropriate for their children.

Majority of games appropriate for everyone

70% of games are appropriate for everyone; only 9% are rated mature (M).

With the demographics of the industry changing rapidly, so too has the type and mix of products published by game companies. Contrary to popular perceptions, most games do not contain significant levels of violence. In fact, the video game rating system the industry voluntarily set up in 1994, and which Sen. Joe Lieberman has repeatedly praised, has rated over 7,500 titles of which only 9% carry a Mature rating. Seventy percent are rated for Everyone over six. In 1999, only 100 out of 1,500 titles released were Mature games, and these represented just 5% of total sales.

Not only are most games appropriate for everyone, but also most of the best sellers are not violent. For example, just from March to September 2000, the top selling games have been Pokemon, Who Wants to Be a Millionaire, SimCity 3000, and racing and skateboarding games. So far in 2000, only two of the top selling PC and video games are rated M, and 16 are rated Everyone. What this reflects is the fact that video games are now mass market entertainment and the range and diversity of products has widened, resulting in a substantial market for casual games like puzzle, board, and card games, and hunting and fishing titles, in addition to staples like racing, football, and action games.

In short, this industry has seen its sales double since 1995. The bulk of that growth has been fueled by consumers over the age of 18 and by games whose content has broad appeal.

Commitment to effective self-regulation

The video and PC game industry has been committed to effective self-regulation since the formation of the IDSA in 1994. We have consistently and continuously sought to respond to concerns about the small number of our products that contain significant violence, balancing our absolute commitment to creative freedom with our commitment to empowering consumers to make informed choices. We are guided by our belief that the ultimate responsibility for controlling the games that come into the home lies with parents—not industry, not Congress, and not federal or state governments. According to the FTC, 45% of parents who are aware of the video game rating system say they do not use it. I submit to you that no one has yet conceived of a law that can mandate sound parenting.

In 1994, the IDSA created the Entertainment Software Rating Board, or ESRB, which uses teams of independent, demographically diverse raters to review each and every video game. ESRB issues ratings suggesting—and that is a key word "suggesting" but not dictating—the age appropriateness of a title. In addition ESRB ratings provide simple but clear information about the content that influenced the rating, such as animated violence, strong language, or suggestive themes. The philosophy underpinning the ESRB system is to give parents the tools to make informed choices, but not to attempt to dictate to them what is right for their families. At the same time the ESRB was created, IDSA voluntarily created an Advertising Code of Conduct requiring that the ratings and content information issued by ESRB be placed on packaging and in advertising. The Ad Code also contained a provision advising that "companies must not specifically target advertising for entertainment software products rated for Teen, Mature, or Adults Only to consumers for whom the product is not rated as appropriate."

[The Interactive Digital Software Association has] consistently and continuously sought to respond to concerns about the small number of our products that contain significant violence.

Starting in 1995, the ESRB maintained an active program to provide information on the ESRB to retailers and consumers. It established a toll free number which has logged millions of calls since its inception, created a multilingual website where consumers can get information on the age and content rating of over 6,000 video games, and distributed millions of Parent Guides to ESRB Ratings to retailers and advocacy throughout the country, as well as to the Attorney General of Illinois.

In 1997, recognizing the emergence of the Internet, the ESRB launched a new rating service called ESRB Interactive, or ESRBi. Through this service, ESRB offers companies the opportunity to rate their websites and video games distributed online. More and more companies are now rating online games and game websites with ESRBi.

The philosophy underpinning the ESRB system is to give parents the tools to make informed choices.

In May 1999, in the weeks after the Columbine tragedy,[1] I appeared before a hearing of this Committee chaired by Sen. Sam Brownback, and made a series of new commitments in response to renewed concerns about entertainment violence. Specifically, IDSA said:

1. it would launch a stepped up campaign to educate consumers about the rating system;
2. we would reach out more aggressively to retailers to encourage them to both increase the amount of rating information available in stores and enforce the ESRB ratings; and
3. we would examine industry advertising practices and explore ways we could address concerns in this area, both as to the content of ads and the targeting of these ads.

We have redeemed every commitment made that day.

Raising consumer and retailer awareness

During the fall of 1999, ESRB launched an extraordinary campaign to raise awareness and use of its ratings, with the centerpiece being a public service announcement (PSA) featuring [professional golfer] Tiger Woods urging parents to "Check the Rating" of games they buy. ESRB purchased advertising in major national publications with significant parent readership, such as *Good Housekeeping*, *Parenting*, and *Newsweek*. ESRB placed pull-out flyers in major parent-oriented publications, such as *Child Magazine*. It redesigned its consumer brochures and distributed millions to leading retailers; and it reached out to leading national grassroots organizations with ties to schools and parents, such as Mothers Against Violence in America and the PTA, seeking ways to partner with them to get the word out to consumers, especially parents, about ESRB ratings and how to use them.

Furthermore, the IDSA sent letters to major national retailers asking them to make a commitment to consumers to use their best efforts not to sell Mature rated games to persons under 17, a step we had also taken in October 1998. As you know, Toys 'R' Us was the first retailer to adopt this policy and in September 2000 K-Mart, Wal-Mart, and Target have done so as well. IDSA supports those efforts. We believe other retailers will soon follow suit.

In addition to all these steps, the IDSA Board this past July renewed its commitment to another paid media campaign this holiday season to

---

1. On April 20, 1999, at Columbine High School in Littleton, Colorado, two student gunmen killed twelve students and a teacher before turning the guns on themselves.

promote the ESRB, and offered to fund 50 percent of the cost of producing in-store educational materials on the ESRB for use by retailers.

Yet another voluntary self-regulatory step came as a result of discussions that began at the White House Summit on Violence. The IDSA and ESRB completed an agreement with America Online (AOL) in which AOL adopted the ESRB ratings as the standard for games on its service. ESRB and AOL have also formed a Task Force to promote the ESRB ratings with other leading Internet sites.

In September 1999, the IDSA Board took the extraordinary and far reaching step of asking the ESRB to create a new Advertising Review Council (ARC) within the ESRB. The ARC is empowered both to ensure that all advertisements by those who use ESRB ratings adhere to strict content standards covering such areas as violence, sex, and language, and to enforce compliance with all other provisions of the industry ad code, including the anti-targeting provision. In addition, the IDSA shifted responsibility for the ad code and its enforcement from the association to the new ESRB ad council, and provided a major increase in resources to support expanded staffing and more aggressive monitoring and enforcement of advertising standards. This initiative was undertaken long before the FTC report was completed, and reflected our own judgment that our industry needed to revamp and step up our approach to monitoring and enforcing our advertising standards. The ARC unit began operations February 1—coincidentally the cutoff date by the FTC's of its monitoring effort—and one of its first successes was convincing virtually every top game enthusiast magazine—the primary advertising vehicle for our industry—to adopt the ARC principles and guidelines as their own. In addition, Ziff-Davis, IDG, and Imagine, the three top publishers of game magazines, sit on the ARC Board of Directors. Since February, ARC has been meeting extensively with IDSA members to educate them on the ad code and ensure compliance.

The most comprehensive system

We appreciate the fact that the FTC described our industry's overall self-regulatory program as "the most comprehensive of the three industry systems studied by the Commission" and that it recognized that "it is widely used by industry members and has been revised repeatedly to address new challenges, developments, and concerns regarding the practices of our members." The FTC also pointed out that quite the opposite of standing by idly, we have been aggressive in seeking compliance with our standards. As it put it, "to its credit, the IDSA has taken several steps to encourage industry members to comply with" the industry's various ratings and advertising requirements. Also perhaps lost in the hubbub over the report is the recognition by the FTC that the independent rating system used by the video game industry "appears to be helpful to those parents who actually use it" and that a majority of these parents say it does an excellent or good job in advising them on the levels of violence in our products.

In this regard, [researcher] Peter Hart completed a new survey July 2000 seeking to gauge whether consumers themselves believe that ESRB ratings are accurate. The research involved mall-intercept interviews with 410 adults nationwide, including 246 parents who were shown videotapes of game clips and asked to rate them based on the ESRB standards. The survey found that "in 84% of all instances, games are rated equal to or less strictly than the official ESRB rating." Hart found that the ESRB is "twice as likely to be more conservative than the public" in rating decisions. With respect to the content descriptors, the survey found "participants are generally in agreement with the ESRB on violence descriptors, and in instances in which there is disagreement, they are usually less strict than the ratings board." In short, the ESRB ratings are reliable and effective.

> *The independent rating system used by the video game industry "appears to be helpful to those parents who actually use it."*

It is clear, though, that the FTC uncovered individual marketing plans [that] indicate that some of our members, in violation of long standing industry guidelines, planned to market, and may have marketed, games rated for Mature users to young people. Let me make it clear to this Committee that the IDSA does not condone or excuse the marketing of Mature rated products to persons under 17 and, indeed, we condemn it. As I noted, six years ago and long before the recent outcry over media violence, we ourselves voluntarily created an advertising code of conduct, which contained an anti-targeting provision.

But it also must be pointed out that we have some legitimate business disagreement with the FTC's analysis of industry practices and the impression the report conveys of our industry's markets and marketing. Thus, let me take a moment to address several facts ignored by the FTC.

Game advertising outlets

According to statistics collected by the ESRB's new Advertising Review Council, since February 1, 2000, the 16 leading game enthusiast magazines, noted by the FTC as the primary vehicles for industry marketing, ran a total of 1,830 ads for games. Of these, only 188, or about 10%, were for Mature rated product. The most M rated ads in a single issue was 7, and typically, each issue contains only 3 or 4 ads for Mature rated products. This relative paucity of ads for M rated product reflects the fact, as I pointed out earlier, that M rated games are actually a small portion of the overall game market both in total releases and retail sales. The question of whether those ads should or should not appear in these publications is a fair point of discussion, but let's all understand that any suggestion that companies are flooding consumers with ads for Mature rated product is simply not accurate.

One of our major quarrels with the FTC report is the apparent assumption that magazines with what it calls "a majority under-17 readership it are not appropriate outlets for advertising of Mature rated games, and that websites or TV shows that are 'popular' with kids are similarly inappropriate outlets for advertising Mature product." We agree that placing an ad for a Mature rated product in a publication that is clearly and squarely aimed at young readers, such as *Nickelodeon* or Sports Illustrated

SI for Kids, is a violation of our standards. But we reject the FTC's operating assumption that ads in publications that happen to have some noteworthy percentage of young readers, but a substantial and perhaps even dominant share of older readers and users, is inappropriate. We do not think it is unreasonable for a company to place an ad for a game in *Game-Pro* magazine where the average age of the readers is 18. We do not feel it is inappropriate to place an M ad in *Electronic Gaming Monthly* (EGM) where, according to the magazine, 59% of its readers are 17 and over. The FTC, by the way, in some apparent zeal to make its point, says its standard for review for game magazines are those with a majority of subscribers age 17 or under. The problem with this, of course, is that an M rated game is appropriate for persons 17 and older so the FTC should have used an under 17 cutoff. It's hard to know how this skews its data but it is clear that in the case of EGM, it makes a dramatic difference.

In the same vein, FTC's use of a "popularity" test to rule out other advertising outlets is restrictive and commercially impractical. "Popularity" is not much of a bright line standard. Using this guidepost, virtually every game website and sites like mtv.com would be off limits to advertisers of Mature products even though a majority of viewers may be in the appropriately targeted demographic group. This is unreasonably restrictive.

The IDSA does not condone or excuse the marketing of Mature rated products to persons under 17.

It's easy to lose sight of the fact, in all the rhetoric and political posturing, that video games are entertainment products for people of all ages, that they are constitutionally protected products, and that at best, the scientific evidence linking them to harmful effects is weak and ambiguous at best, and at worst does not exist. Indeed, that's exactly what The Government of Australia concluded in December 1999 after an exhaustive evaluation of all the available research on violent video games.

The Australian Government report concluded: "After examining several attempts to find effects of aggressive content in either experimental studies or field studies, at best only weak and ambiguous evidence has emerged. Importantly these studies have employed current games or concerned contemporary young players who presumably have access to the latest games. The accumulating evidence—provided largely by researchers keen to demonstrate the games' undesirable effects—does indicate that it is very hard to find such effects and that they are unlikely to be substantial.". . .

Parents' watchdog role

I will not tell you our industry has been perfect either in its conduct or its implementation of our own standards. I will tell you we have shown a genuine commitment to the principle of informing consumers about the content of our products and regulating how these products are marketed. We have proven that with or without the FTC, with or without the heat of a presidential campaign, our efforts to continue to enhance our self-regulatory regime are unwavering.

At the same time, we must acknowledge that we do live in a world where media is incredibly complex, where the Internet spans the globe, where consumers, young and old, have access to information in ways never before imagined. In this environment, it is simply not possible or realistic to create an air-tight system where young people do not hear about, or even obtain, games that are not appropriate for them. To the extent this occurs due to industry's unambiguous effort to target kids to buy M rated products, it is not defensible. But to the extent it happens as a result of the information and media explosion flooding over all of us, it is unfair and unrealistic to point fingers.

Where does this leave us? About where the FTC said when it commented on parents' awareness of the rating system. "It is clear that most parents are able to play a watchdog role when they choose to do so. . . . [The] level of parental involvement, either at the point of selection or purchase, means that most parents have the opportunity to review rating information or to check the product packaging to determine whether they approve of the game's content."

In the final analysis, we all must work cooperatively to ensure that parents know about and make use of the rating systems. In a world where nearly half say they do not even pay attention to the efforts our industry already makes, it seems to me that is a goal we all can work towards.

5

Video Games Are an Emerging Art

Henry Jenkins

Henry Jenkins is director of the program in Comparative Media Studies at the Massachusetts Institute of Technology.

Video games must be taken seriously as an art because they exhibit the artistic capabilities of computer technology. The inventive cinematic qualities of movement and space in video games have influenced contemporary cutting-edge films. However, the potential for artistic expression in video games is weighed down by the banality, predictability, and violence that characterize most games. Critics and the public should give the art of video games room to mature and constructively criticize the elements they find objectionable.

Are video games a massive drain on our income, time and energy? A new form of "cultural pollution," as one U.S. senator described them? The "nightmare before Christmas," in the words of another? Are games teaching our children to kill, as countless op-ed pieces have warned?

No. Computer games are art—a popular art, an emerging art, a largely unrecognized art, but art nevertheless.

From Pong to Final Fantasy

Over the past 25 years, games have progressed from the primitive two-paddles-and-a-ball Pong to the sophistication of Final Fantasy, a participatory story with cinema-quality graphics that unfolds over nearly 100 hours of play. The computer game has been a killer app [application] for the home PC, increasing consumer demand for vivid graphics, rapid processing, greater memory and better sound. The release this fall of the Sony Playstation 2, coupled with the announcement of next-generation consoles by Nintendo and Microsoft, signals a dramatic increase in the resources available to game designers.

Games increasingly influence contemporary cinema, helping to define the frenetic pace and model the multi-directional plotting of *Run Lola Run*, providing the role-playing metaphor for *Being John Malkovich* and encouraging a fascination with the slippery line between reality and digital illusion in *The Matrix*. At high schools and colleges across the country, students discuss games with the same passions with which earlier generations debated the merits of the New American Cinema. Media studies programs report a growing number of their students want to be game designers rather than filmmakers.

The time has come to take games seriously as an important new popular art shaping the aesthetic sensibility of the 21st century. I will admit that discussing the art of video games conjures up comic images: tuxedo-clad and jewel-bedecked patrons admiring the latest Streetfighter, middle-aged academics pontificating on the impact of Cubism on Tetris, bleeps and zaps disrupting our silent contemplation at the Guggenheim. Such images tell us more about our contemporary notion of art—as arid and stuffy, as the property of an educated and economic elite, as cut off from everyday experience—than they tell us about games. . . .

The computer is simply a tool, one that offers artists new resources and opportunities for reaching the public; it is human creativity that makes art. Still, one can only imagine how the critics would have responded to the idea that something as playful, unpretentious and widely popular as a computer game might be considered art.

The time has come to take [video] games seriously as an important new popular art shaping the aesthetic sensibility of the 21st century.

In 1925, leading literary and arts critic Gilbert Seldes took a radical approach to the aesthetics of popular culture in a treatise titled *The Seven Lively Arts*. Adopting what was then a controversial position, Seldes argued that America's primary contributions to artistic expression had come through emerging forms of popular culture such as jazz, the Broadway musical, the Hollywood cinema and the comic strip. While these arts have gained cultural respectability over the past 75 years, each was disreputable when Seldes staked out his position.

A new lively art

Cinema and other popular arts were to be celebrated, Seldes said, because they were so deeply imbedded in everyday life, because they were democratic arts embraced by average citizens. Through streamlined styling and syncopated rhythms, they captured the vitality of contemporary urban experience. They took the very machinery of the industrial age, which many felt dehumanizing, and found within it the resources for expressing individual visions, for reasserting basic human needs, desires and fantasies. And these new forms were still open to experimentation and discovery. They were, in Seldes' words, "lively arts."

Games represent a new lively art, one as appropriate for the digital age as those earlier media were for the machine age. They open up new aesthetic experiences and transform the computer screen into a realm of experimentation and innovation that is broadly accessible. And games have been embraced by a public that has otherwise been unimpressed by much of what passes for digital art. Much as the salon arts of the 1920s seemed sterile alongside the vitality and inventiveness of popular culture, contemporary efforts to create interactive narrative through modernist hypertext or avant-garde installation art seem lifeless and pretentious alongside the creativity that game designers bring to their craft.

[Video games] open up new aesthetic experiences and transform the computer screen into a realm of experimentation and innovation that is broadly accessible.

Much of what Seldes told us about the silent cinema seems remarkably apt for thinking about games. Silent cinema, he argued, was an art of expressive movement. He valued the speed and dynamism of [director] D.W. Griffith's last-minute races to the rescue, the physical grace of Charlie Chaplin's pratfalls and the ingenuity of Buster Keaton's engineering feats. Games also depend upon an art of expressive movement, with characters defined through their distinctive ways of propelling themselves through space, and successful products structured around a succession of spectacular stunts and predicaments. Will future generations look back on Lara Croft doing battle with a pack of snarling wolves as the 21st-century equivalent of [actor] Lillian Gish making her way across the ice floes in *Way Down East*? The art of silent cinema was also an art of atmospheric design. To watch a silent masterpiece like [director] Fritz Lang's *Metropolis* is to be drawn into a world where meaning is carried by the placement of shadows, the movement of machinery and the organization of space. If anything, game designers have pushed beyond cinema in terms of developing expressive and fantastic environments that convey a powerful sense of mood, provoke our curiosity and amusement, and motivate us to explore.

Why should pixels be different?

In the March 6, 2000 issue of *Newsweek*, senior editor Jack Kroll argued that audiences will probably never be able to care as deeply about pixels on the computer screen as they care about characters in films: "Moviemakers don't have to simulate human beings; they are right there, to be recorded and orchestrated. . . . The top-heavy titillation of Tomb Raider's Lara Croft falls flat next to the face of Sharon Stone. . . . Any player who's moved to tumescence by digibimbo Lara is in big trouble." Yet countless viewers cry when Bambi's mother dies, and World War II veterans can tell you they felt real lust for *Esquire*'s Vargas girls. We have learned to care as much about creatures of pigment as we care about images of real people. Why should pixels be different?

In the end, games may not take the same path as cinema. Game designers will almost certainly develop their own aesthetic principles as they confront the challenge of balancing our competing desires for storytelling and interactivity. It remains to be seen whether games can provide players the freedom they want and still provide an emotionally satisfying and thematically meaningful shape to the experience. Some of the best games—Tetris comes to mind—have nothing to do with storytelling. For all we know, the future art of games may look more like architecture or dance than cinema. . . .

The problem with most contemporary games isn't that they are violent but that they are banal, formulaic and predictable. Thoughtful criticism can marshal support for innovation and experimentation in the industry, much as good film criticism helps focus attention on neglected independent films. Thoughtful criticism could even contribute to our debates about game violence. So far, the censors and culture warriors have gotten more or less a free ride because we almost take for granted that games are culturally worthless. We should instead look at games as an emerging art form—one that does not simply simulate violence but increasingly offers new ways to understand violence—and talk about how to strike a balance between this form of expression and social responsibility. Moreover, game criticism may provide a means of holding the game industry more accountable for its choices. In the wake of the Columbine shootings,[1] game designers are struggling with their ethical responsibilities as never before, searching for ways of appealing to empowerment fantasies that don't require exploding heads and gushing organs. A serious public discussion of this medium might constructively influence these debates, helping identify and evaluate alternatives as they emerge.

A maturing art

As the art of games matures, progress will be driven by the most creative and forward-thinking minds in the industry, those who know that games can be more than they have been, those who recognize the potential of reaching a broader public, of having a greater cultural impact, of generating more diverse and ethically responsible content and of creating richer and more emotionally engaging stories. But without the support of an informed public and the perspective of thoughtful critics, game developers may never realize that potential.

---

1. On April 20, 1999, at Columbine High School in Littleton, Colorado, two student gunmen killed twelve students and a teacher before turning the guns on themselves.

6

"Emotion Engine"?
I Don't Think So

Jack Kroll

The late Jack Kroll was a noted arts and entertainment critic and a longtime editor at Newsweek.

Video game designers are convinced that their games have artistic value. They believe that the pioneers of their industry should be seated among the world's greatest and most influential artists. However, even the most sophisticated video games cannot evoke the emotional complexity of art. Images contrived by digital technology merely represent the manipulation of mechanics and cannot convey the essence of humanity.

Why can't these game wizards be satisfied with their ingenuity, their $7 billion (and rising) in sales, their capture of a huge chunk of youth around the world? Why must they claim that what they are doing is "art"? And should anyone care whether this emerging medium is art or not? The point is, the game designers care. They lust after the title of Artist. You might think these cutting-edge, post-post-everything guys would scorn such an ancient calling. Not so; you don't hear them boasting, "We've gone beyond art. Art is moldy old stuff for moldy old people." No, they need art, because, being very intelligent, they know that art is crucial, that human beings and art have had a—what's that buzzword?—synergistic relationship from the beginning, from the prehistoric cave paintings to Homer to Shakespeare to Mozart to Tolstoy to Charlie Chaplin to Picasso to Robert Frost to Louis Armstrong to Balanchine to Fred Astaire. Phil Harrison, vice president of research and development for PlayStation, foresees "a game designer in the future who can have the social impact of a great movie director, author or musician." Game masters like Harrison know all about the history of art, which is the history of humankind's ceaseless attempts to grasp and express the meaning of the world and their own nature.

That's a pretty highfalutin statement, but if you want to be in the art business, you have to falute pretty high. As digital games have increased

in technical power, their creators have been swept into a kind of eupho-
ria. Sony research director Dominic Mallinson says that games are moving
away from basic "stimulus and response" toward "creativity and performance." He talks of "cognitive modeling" which can produce intelligent
dinosaurs, and "particle rendering" which can simulate things like smoke
and tornadoes. He foresees games' reaching such technical sophistication
that they could "create a script on the fly." But even Mallinson admits
that a game "never can do it the way a human being can do it." And it's
human beings who create art, not the polygons and Bezier curves of digital technology.

---

*Computer games create a world of manipulative
mechanics, without the catharsis and revelation of
real art.*

Games can be fun and rewarding in many ways, but they can't transmit the emotional complexity that is the root of art. Even the most ad-
vanced games lack the shimmering web of nuances that makes human
life different from mechanical process. Interestingly, movies can transmit
the sense of this nuanced complexity where games cannot. Moviemakers
don't have to simulate human beings; they are right there, to be recorded
and orchestrated. The digitally created medieval Japanese warriors in
Kessen (one of the first titles made for PlayStation 2) have none of the
breathing presence, the epic gallantry, of the knights in Akira Kurosawa's
1985 film *Ran*. The top-heavy titillation of Tomb Raider's Lara Croft falls
flat next to the face of Sharon Stone, smiling with challenging sensuality
at some haplessly macho male in *Basic Instinct*. Any player who's moved
to tumescence by digibimbo Lara is in big trouble.

Games have their own importance in cultural history. In his book
Homo Ludens—Man the Game-Player—the Dutch sociologist Johan
Huizinga writes that play predated religion and culture; play "creates order." On the other hand, he says that "solitary play" is of little consequence, "sharpening the mental faculties very one-sidedly without en-
riching the soul in any way." The millions sitting at their consoles and
computers would no doubt have made Huizinga one depressed Dutch-
man, even if they were interacting with others sitting at their consoles
from Munich to Mandalay.

The question of whether computer games are art is part of the larger
debate about the effect of the accelerating interaction between humans
and machines. "Our goal is to come up with an algorithmic definition of
creativity," wrote artificial-intelligence (AI) researchers Roger Schank and
Christopher Owens, insisting that the artist merely has "a certain set of
cognitive skills" that computers will inevitably acquire. Another AI man,
Raymond Kurzweil, awaits the coming of "artificial people . . . life-size
three-dimensional images with sufficiently high resolution . . . to be in-
distinguishable from real people."

But behind such techno-magic lies a banality of vision and style.
Computer games create a world of manipulative mechanics, without the
catharsis and revelation of real art. The scary thing is the seductiveness of

this world, especially for young people, for whom it is natural to be citizens of a culture of games. This is a new breed, perhaps even a new evolutionary event in the species. Sitting at their joysticks, they await the coming of Phil Harrison's envisioned savior, someone who can shatter the Pavlovian world of stimulus and response, and create a genuine new art from those patterned puppets on a world of screens.

7

Joy Sick; Games Can Be an Addiction

Jon Tevlin

Jon Tevlin is a reporter for the Minneapolis Star Tribune.

For 6 to 10 percent of video game enthusiasts, playing video games could lead to genuine addiction. Compulsive video game users become dependent on video games to help them ignore their real-life problems. Others become addicted because game playing allows them to adopt other personalities, which enhances their self-esteem. Video game addicts also crave the adrenaline rush they experience from playing games. As with other addictions, unhealthy obsessions with video games have damaged people's lives and ruined relationships.

B y day, Matt Gillen is a project manager for a company. By night, he's a wood elf druid named Leaff Samhain who wanders through a virtual kingdom, often meeting with other wood elves or tangling with barbarian warriors.

These nights, Gillen is by himself at his home computer. But he is not alone.

Hooked on "Evercrack"

As many as 40,000 people are with him on servers around the globe, engaged in a three-dimensional online game called Everquest. Since its arrival in computer stores in spring 1999, the game has sold 250,000 copies, making it the most popular game of its kind.

In fact, the game is so popular and time-consuming that it has been dubbed "Evercrack" by those hooked on it. Gillen controls his playing time but understands how some people could get addicted—he once played for 16 hours straight.

During the recent holiday season, millions of people received computer games such as Everquest, and psychologists say as many as 10 percent could become addicted to the games.

James Fearing, president of National Counseling Intervention Services in Plymouth, Minn., says computer-game obsessions have damaged relationships and caused students to fail their courses. Some people get so hooked on games and the Internet that family interventions are called for. Fearing has even sent people to 30-day inpatient treatments for computer addictions.

Fearing has been receiving more and more calls about computer-game obsessions and other calls from people who can't control their use of Internet chat rooms.

He thinks the phenomenon is being underreported. "I see a lot of denial, the same as in other addictions," he said. "And people don't recognize yet that a person who is unable to control their use of the computer has the same by-products as a drug user."

Considerable research has concluded that computer games can help people develop skills, such as concentration and problem-solving. They also can offer worthwhile benign entertainment.

Games' dark side

But Fearing and others say there can be a "dark side" to such games for 6 percent to 10 percent of users. "Families of addicted people often feel like they are in competition with the computer," said Fearing. "In marriages, it's almost as if there's another person in the relationship."

According to Fearing, people retreat into computer games or online diversions for three reasons:

Avoidance. "The person is trying to ignore other problems, such as marital strife or financial trouble. Like drug addicts, they are creating a world free from stress, pain and worry," Fearing said.

Sexual fantasy. It's usually seen in people hooked on Internet pornography or chat rooms, Fearing said, but it also plays a role in games that often feature scantily clad women and provocative conversations—such as Everquest.

Fantasy. The person escapes, or gains self esteem, by adopting online personalities. You can be an airline pilot one minute, and 15 minutes later you can be CEO of a company, or a warrior.

Gillen, who lives in Minneapolis, says that's what draws many to Everquest.

Computer-game obsessions have damaged relationships and caused students to fail their courses.

"I know it sounds silly to someone outside the game, but when you get into it you find it is kind of like another world that allows you to do something you can't do in real life," he said. "People may not be successful or feel like they are moving up in real life, but there are those four hours when they are playing the game. It gives you a real sense of power. And it feels real."

Messages from an Everquest newsgroup:

"I found dumping the women is about the easiest way to find time to play, I play from 6 P.M. to 12 or 1 A.M. every night. Sacrifices are needed if you want to be high-level."

"I played nearly nonstop the entire weekend. I couldn't imagine ever NOT playing the game. I'm wondering if I should let my account lapse or not. It's not just me, either, from the posts I've seen."

"The adrenaline rush a game player gets is not unlike the one a gambler gets."

Researchers are unsure if problems or personality disorders are shared by the woman who spends days in a chat room, the man addicted to Internet porn, and the kid obsessed with Everquest, according to work on the subject by Maressa Hecht Orzack, a Harvard University psychologist and director of Computer Addiction Services at McLean Hospital in Belmont, Mass.

"Most people who start out don't realize they'll have a problem," said Fearing. "But an invisible line is crossed, and pretty soon their whole life is out of balance."

Always available

Unlike other addictions, Fearing said, "you don't have to go to a liquor store or a drug dealer or a casino. You just have to walk into another room."

Role-playing games such as Everquest run worldwide around the clock, so it's always available. And, like heroin, the first taste (month) is free.

Fearing's case list includes a woman who recently called with concerns about her son, a former honor student who was failing his college courses because he spent so much time playing computer games.

One couple split up over the wife's online obsession.

"They had just built their dream house together," said Fearing. "The husband told her to get rid of the computer or get out. She took the computer."

Treatments are similar to those used in drug addiction. Fearing once gathered the family around a woman who would not leave her computer. They explained how her obsession was affecting their lives.

Like other addictions, computer and computer-game obsessions cut across the lines of race, age, education and income, although psychologists so far have found a higher incidence among highly educated white males with good incomes.

"Being on the computer a lot doesn't make you an addict, just like drinking a lot doesn't necessarily make you an alcoholic," said Fearing. "The No. 1 symptom is a loss of control, an inability to self-regulate."

Some addicted players quit "cold turkey." Others are taught to set limits. Harvard's Orzack makes "contracts" with people to help them limit their computer time.

In the worst cases, Fearing sends patients to 30-day inpatient treatments similar to those found at Hazelden. Two programs in Arizona and one in Texas specialize in computer-related addictions. Computer addiction, however, is not yet recognized by insurers as a disease, so clients must pay their own way.

Laura Gurak, an associate professor of rhetoric at the University of Minnesota who is setting up a Center for Internet Studies and working on a book about the Internet, has heard students discuss the allure of Everquest and other games.

"I've also heard people talk about how addictive Myst is," she said, referring to another computer game. "I could see how it could be different from other addictions because of the incredible graphics and amazing sound. The more fantastic the world is, the more the appeal."

Fearing said that "the adrenaline rush a game player gets is not unlike the one a gambler gets."

For Everquest fanatics, moving up through the 50 levels of the visually rich 3-D game and acquiring virtual treasures such as swords, belts and kingdoms is so valued that those who can't afford the time can even buy these items from other game players in Internet auctions: virtual property for real cash (sometimes up to $1,500).

Not the gamemaker's fault

The game's maker, 989 Studios, has heard people joke about Everquest compulsion, but the company downplays potential negative effects. Spokesmen said that "hard-core" fans spend six to 10 hours on the game in a day.

"It's a great game," said Helene Sheler, director of public relations and promotions for 989 Studios. "No matter how much you play, you can't ever really master it. We're happy that people like to play it."

Fearing said that addiction is not the gamemaker's fault: "I don't blame Budweiser for alcoholics, either. It's about responsible use."

8

Playing Video Games Benefits Children

David Deutsch

David Deutsch is a noted British physicist and author of The Fabric of
Reality.

Video games are highly beneficial because they give children a
unique interactive learning environment. The interactive element
of video games benefits children because it imparts the fundamental thinking skills needed for creativity and problem solving.
Playing video games is inherently similar to interactive activities
such as chess or playing the piano except that video games are
stigmatized and those other educational activities are not. The
stigmatization of video games ultimately discourages children
from learning.

Far from believing computer games to be harmful, [author and physi-
cist] David Deutsch believes them to be very *good* for children. Inter-
viewer Sarah Lawrence asked him what is so good about computer games.

David Deutsch: In a way, that is the wrong question, because it as-
sumes that there is something obviously *bad* about video games, which
might be offset by benefits I might mention. But there's nothing wrong
with video games. So let's ask first, "Why do so many adults hate them?
What *evidence* is there that there is anything bad about them?"

If you look at it closely, the evidence boils down to no more than the
fact that children *like* video games. There seems to be a very common tendency among parents to regard children *liking* something as *prima facie*
evidence that it is bad for them. If they are spending a lot of time doing
something, parents wonder what harm it must be doing them. I think
this is fundamentally the wrong attitude.

The right attitude is: if children are spending a lot of time doing something, let's try to find ways of letting them do *even more* of it. *Prima facie*,
the fact that they like doing it is an indication that it is good for them.

I think that overwhelmingly the thing which draws people's attention to video games is the fact that children like them. People jump from

that solitary piece of evidence to the conclusion that there must be some-thing wrong with video games!

As it happens, I believe that playing video games is very good for you but, I think, even more important than understanding why it is good for you, is to understand and avoid the temptation of saying that if you like it, it must be bad for you.

Now, why is playing video games good for you? They provide a unique learning environment. They provide something which for most of human history was not available, namely, an interactive complex entity that is accessible at low cost and zero risk.

Video games are a breakthrough in human culture.

Let's compare video games with other great educational things in the world. Books and television have great complexity and diversity—they give you access to almost every aspect of human culture and knowledge—but they are not interactive. On the other hand, something like playing the piano is also complex, and interactive, but it requires an enormous initial investment (months or years of practice or training) with the asso-ciated huge risk of misplacing that investment. One cannot make many such investments in one's life. I should say, of course, that *the* most edu-cational thing in the world is conversation. That does have the property that it is complex, interactive, and ought to have a low cost, although of-ten between children and adults it has a high cost and high risk for the children, but it should not and need not.

Apart from conversation, all the complex interactive things require a huge initial investment, except video games, and I think video games are a breakthrough in human culture for that reason. They are not some tran-sient, fringe aspect of culture; they are destined to be an important means of human learning for the rest of history, because of this interactive ele-ment. Why is being interactive so important? Because interacting with a complex entity is what life and thinking and creativity and art and sci-ence are all about.

Understanding a complex and autonomous world

Sarah Lawrence: In The Face *magazine (December 1992, page 46), Dr Mar-garet Shotton, author of* Computer Addiction?, *is quoted as saying, "Apart from increasing your manual dexterity and hand to eye coordination, video games speed up your neural pathways." This, the writer says, allows knowledge to travel around quicker, thus speeding up judgements and decisions, possibly leading to a higher IQ. Margaret Shotton, like David Deutsch, believes that par-ents who disapprove of their children playing computer games are mistaken, but David Deutsch is sceptical about the neural pathways theory. Perhaps surpris-ingly, he doubts that computer games improve hand-eye coordination.*

Life improves one's hand-eye coordination. One spends one's whole life picking things up and doing fine finger movements, which one does in video games as well, but video games, if they are well designed, tend to use skills which people already have. If they go too far beyond what people already have, they tend to be less attractive as video games. They are then more like playing the piano, which requires a new kind of physical skill. Video games do not really impart a new kind of physical skill; what they impart is *the* fundamental *mental* skill, of understanding a complex and autonomous world.

Many parents would agree that conversation is very valuable, and it is because their children spend so many hours playing computer games instead of conversing, that they worry.

I do not accept that children play video games *instead* of conversation. They love both, and there is plenty of time in a day for many hours of video games and many hours of conversation—especially since, in my experience, it is perfectly possible to play video games and talk at the same time. Most parents do not talk enough to their children. If they want to talk to their children, let them do so. If the conversation is interesting enough, the children will talk. They will either talk during the video game or, if it is *very* interesting, they may postpone the video game. Forcing them to give up the video game in order to talk will make the resulting conversation worthless.

Number of hours playing games

Could the number of hours children spend playing computer games be harmful?

Let me answer that question in two ways. First, how do you know what the appropriate number of hours is? Nobody can know that. If your children were playing chess for several hours a day, you would boast about what geniuses they are. There is no intrinsic difference between chess and a video game, or indeed, even between things like playing the piano and playing video games, except that playing the piano has this enormous initial cost. They are similar kinds of activity. One of them is culturally sanctioned and the other is still culturally stigmatised, but for no good reason. I spent a lot of time playing with Lego when I was a child. For some reason, it never occurred to my parents that because I spent hours and hours with Lego, this was bad for me. If it had occurred to them, they could have done a lot of harm. I know now, for myself, that the thing which makes me play video games today is identical to the thing which made me play with Lego then—which is, by the way, the very same thing that makes me do science—that is, the impulse to understand things.

What [video games] impart is the *fundamental* mental *skill, of understanding a complex and autonomous world.*

Could it be harmful? Suppose a child is for some reason unhappy with his situation—his home life or school or whatever—and he has very few creative outlets. Playing video games is such a good thing in this respect, that if he finds it, and finds other avenues blocked off, he may devote all his attention to it. Later, if his circumstances change, he may not be as open to taking up other opportunities as he might have been. If that is so, it is not the video game that is doing him harm, it is that he has been funnelled down a blind alley and not let out. The thing to do is to let him out, not to steal his last remaining source of joy and learning. If someone is in that state, just like with any compulsive behaviour, the cure is simply to offer him other things which he might prefer. There will be *some* things which he prefers; nobody actually spends twenty-four hours a day playing video games so, in the remaining time, try conversation, try anything. If that does not work, don't blame the video game. Be thankful that there is still something good in the child's life, to tide him over.

There is no intrinsic difference between chess and a video game.

But such cases are exceptional. On the whole, if we are talking about how the overwhelming majority of children interact with video games, the reason they sit in front of them for hours is that they are very valuable things to sit in front of. The skills they are learning are needed in every creative aspect of life, and children will always be short of opportunities to learn them. The natural and healthy state of human beings is that we are constantly looking for opportunities to improve our thinking skills, to improve the complexity and the subtlety of the mental apparatus which we apply to the world. Traditionally, this has been expensive, but people still did it. Even learning to play chess is expensive, compared with learning to play a video game. The expense does not make it any more moral. It is a disadvantage of chess or playing the piano that they have this initial cost.

One of the ways you can tell that playing video games is not something which captures people and then holds them to their detriment is that each video game has only a finite lifetime. Video game playing almost always follows a definite pattern. People try a video game, and they tell with one or two playings of it whether this is for them or not. If they like it, they tend to continue to play it for as long as they are still improving. The instant they are no longer improving, they stop, and they go on to another game. That is neither random behaviour, nor any kind of mechanical, Pavlovian or compulsive behaviour. It is typical learning behaviour: you are improving at something, and, so long as you are improving, you carry on doing it; the moment you stop improving, you stop doing it.

You might say, okay, you are learning something, but what you are learning is not really very useful. But that is to misunderstand the whole point of the video game. The benefit of a video game is not that you learn the video game; it is that you learn the mental skills *with which* you are learning the video game, and *those* skills are good for learning *anything*.

The element of violence

Could the element of violence present in many video games be harmful?. . .

Some of my favourite games are "shoot-em-up" games—perhaps I'm just old-fashioned. But *whatever* the type of game, it is not *violence*. Violence is where you hurt people. Games just appear on a screen; they don't actually hurt anybody. The only actual hurting that goes on is by parents when they prevent or discourage children from playing.

All games need an object and, if there are people in the game, it is natural to have drama, which means there will be goodies and baddies. The same is true in all drama, in all novels, plays, films, or whatever. If *King Lear* were the first play a person had seen, he might come out severely shocked. But once you know what a play is, have seen a bit of Shakespeare and know what it is about, you know that *King Lear* is not actually dangerous, that people don't go around after seeing *King Lear*, plucking people's eyes out. People are not harmed by seeing *King Lear* if they have reached the stage of wanting to see it gradually, at their own pace, for their own reasons, under their own control. Video games are *par excellence* a learning environment that is under one's own control, and that prevents them from being harmful.

Somebody made the point to me that playing computer games arouses the fight or flight impulse, and gives children too much excess energy. This idea apparently came from the book Four Arguments for the Elimination of Television. *Parents do worry that seeing violence on screen is much more damaging than seeing violence in a play because video games appear to draw people in very deeply and make them addicted.*

I think that is completely untrue. The only evidence that video games are addictive is that people play them. All this talk about "excess energy" or being "drawn in" and so on is not what scientists would call experimental data. The data are that the child is playing the video game. That is the only thing you know for a *fact*. You can't see this "drawn in" business. That is just an *interpretation* parents put on what has happened. Pure theory, based on their own preconceptions. I am not making a value judgement here. I am just stating a fact. My *judgement* is that these preconceptions are wrong and that children play video games because they instinctively recognise their educational value.

> *Video games are* par excellence *a learning environment that is under one's own control, and that prevents them from being harmful.*

When you play video games, you are using the *emotional* part of your mind as well, because when you interact with complex external entities, you engage your emotions as well as your intellect. Anything worth doing engages the emotions. What would you say about somebody who learned to play the piano, but never got emotionally involved? I remember once, I came back to playing the Appassionata after a long time, and I ended up with blood all over the keys. (It was not as bad as it sounds.) I saw that I had a cut, but I did not want to stop, so I carried on playing. If that had been a video game and I had been younger, people would have used that as evidence of addiction.

Perhaps children feel violent when they are forced to stop playing, and quite right too! Of course somebody who does not like television is likely to be prejudiced against video games, because they are related. Television has advantages, namely, that it is a more diverse opening to culture. On the other hand, it is not interactive. Video games are interactive, but they are less diverse. They both have their strengths and weaknesses.

Sexism in games

Should we be concerned about the sexism in some games?

The way to combat false ideas is not to censor them but to contradict them. Most of the great literature of the world is sexist, and more generally, riddled with all sorts of false and irrational ideas, as well as valuable ones. Nobody would want to cut himself off from all culture just because it is "something-ist." The sexism of some video games is a minor and easily corrected fault. Once you have pointed out to your child how silly it is, she will be able to recognise sexism in other contexts.

I think one thing that is sinister is how boys play video games much more than girls. This is part of the same phenomenon that makes girls reluctant to do science, reluctant to go into management and business, reluctant to do anything creative and effective in the world. It is an effect down a long chain of cause and effect which began with things like being dressed in pink costumes when they were babies. The whole pattern of behaviour towards a girl rewards her for suppressing her creativity. One of the unpleasant side effects of this is that it makes girls suppress the side of them that would like video games. The reason why this effect is more marked in video games is that video games are so well suited for developing creative skills.

People are so much more complicated than these simplistic theories of what "influences" them. Human beings are not laboratory rats, and do not react like laboratory rats. Look at Eastern Europe, where they used to control what everybody read, and gave them a constant diet of Marxist propaganda, which they had to learn by heart in school, and repeat with eagerness in their voices: in spite of all that, it did not rub off on the overwhelming majority of them, and even *those* people are rapidly regretting it. The children went to school; they learned the stuff the same way chil dren do everywhere. The fact that it was Marxist propaganda did not make it any more or less easy to swallow than what children are taught in *our* schools, but it did not go in, any more than what children are taught in *our* schools goes in.

I think that all these fears are *a posteriori*—you first know the conclusion, which is that you must stop him playing the video game, and then you invent the reasons. The reason why video games are hated is that they are, in the true sense, educational. Of course people don't put it like that, but that is what it comes down to.

"Educational" games

Most parents are really very keen to educate their children. Many have no objection to educational games.

But they have a preconception, a vision, of what education must look like, which results largely from psychological injuries inflicted on them in their own childhood in the name of education. They make the fundamental mistake of human relationships, which is to try to use *force* to make the other person act out your vision of him, instead of looking to see who the other person actually is, and what he wants, and trying to help him *get* what he wants. The market tends to do the latter—it tends to do the right thing—and so games which are made for money tend to be good for you. A video game which is designed to be "educational," like everything which is designed to be "educational," tends to be bad. It is making that fundamental error of trying to channel children into a pre-determined vision.

Looking at this more broadly, learning to read is an educational video game. Learning to play a musical instrument is an educational video game. Some of these good things by accident have got social sanction. If children get "addicted" to *those* things, parents overflow with pride. But there is no better criterion for finding out whether something is good for you than whether you enjoy it. There can't be.

[Austrian philosopher] Sir Karl Popper once said "the belief that truth is manifest is the basis of all tyranny." The fact is, the truth is not manifest. The truth can only be found by a critical process, by a creative process, by a process that is open, and our only criterion for whether one idea is better than another is whether we prefer it. We have to *look* at the ideas, and use criticism—everything must be open to criticism—to find which of them is ultimately preferable. We have to be willing to change and change again. If you have a power structure where a single idea of what is right is imposed by force, then that can never be criticised, and the chances of approaching the truth are nil.

Children playing video games—regardless of subject matter—are learning. Adults who prevent this are preventing them from learning.

But there is a whole world out there for children to find out about, to explore. . . .

 And I suppose that's why people lock them up in schools! Even home educating parents tend not to allow their children enough access to the world, just as schooling parents don't. Anyway, the video game world is a complex autonomous world. It is an artificial world, but then so is the street outside. The point is not *what* world you are learning about, but that you are learning *how* to understand the world.

9

Many Video Games Reinforce Gender Stereotypes

Children Now

Children Now is an independent, nonpartisan organization that promotes the welfare of children.

A recent study has indicated that gender stereotypes pervade most video games. For instance, 35 percent of the male characters in the study had extremely muscular bodies, while 20 percent of the female characters had extremely thin or disproportionate bodies. Many female characters also dressed provocatively. Additionally, video game stereotypes may be reinforcing sexist behavioral expectations. In the study, male characters were predominantly agents of action while half of the female characters were passive. These findings highlight the potential for video games to send unhealthy messages to children.

A growing topic of research and debate has centered on the issue of video games and gender. There is great concern about the ways that females are portrayed in video games and the effect that these portrayals can have on young girls' self-image as well as boys' expectations of and attitudes towards females. There is also increasing concern about the kinds of messages that video games send to boys about masculinity, such as the appropriateness of expressing their emotions, the acceptable ways of dealing with conflict, the treatment of women and the ideal male body size.

What types of messages do the portrayal of male and female video game characters send to young players? What types of behaviors are modeled as appropriate for boys and girls? Are games perpetuating gender stereotypes, such as the helpless female and the brave, stoic male?

The male and female populations

• *Female characters accounted for a small minority of characters in video games.* Of the 1716 total characters analyzed in this study, male human characters totaled 1106 (64%) while female human characters numbered only 283 (17%). On average, 17 males appeared in each game, compared to only four females. In addition, more than half of the 70 games in the study featured two or fewer female characters.

• *Females were even less likely to be player-controlled characters.* Of the 874 player-controlled characters, 635 (73%) were males, and only 107 (12%) were females. Players are more likely to have an opportunity to play a non-human character than a female.

Female characters accounted for a small minority of characters in video games.

• *Why are player-controlled characters important?* Player-controlled characters are those characters whom players can usually choose and whose actions they navigate and manipulate through the course of the game. Player-controlled characters are important since they are the characters that players "become" and with whom they are more likely to identify.

• *Males were far more likely than females to appear as player-controlled characters.* Sixty of the seventy games (86%) offered male player-controlled characters while only 36 games (51%) contained even one female character for players to control. Twenty-five games featured only male player-controlled characters, yet only two games (both Tomb Raider titles) featured exclusively female choices.

Character roles

Half of all female characters were props or bystanders while male characters were predominantly competitors. While the primary role for male characters was competitor (47%), the primary role for females was that of prop (32%). Props are characters that provide useful information to the player, but do not engage in any action. In addition, 18% of female human characters were bystanders, or characters that spoke but did not even provide any useful information or resources. Combined, this means that 50% of the female characters did not engage in the action at all.

• *Female player-controlled characters were less likely than males to be competitors and more likely to be participants.* Seven out of ten (70%) male

Top Male Player-Controlled Character Roles			Top Female Player-Controlled Character Roles		
Role	*Number*	*Percent*	*Role*	*Number*	*Percent*
Competitor	445	70%	Competitor	40	37%
Wrestler/Fighter	114	18%	Wrestler/Fighter	25	24%
Hero/Rescuer	38	6%	Hero/Rescuer	11	11%
Participant	22	3%	Participant	23	22%
Villain/Assassin	9	1%	Villain/Assassin	3	3%
Killer/Combatant	7	1%	Killer/Combatant	3	3%

player-controlled characters assumed the role of competitor, while just over one third of female player-controlled characters (37%) had the same role. Females were also seven times more likely to be participants (22%) than were males (3%). Participants are characters that obey the commands of the player, but do not necessarily have personalities or abilities of their own.

Gender stereotyping

• *Female and male characters behaved in different and often stereotypical ways.* Male characters were more likely than females to engage in physical aggression (52% and 32%, respectively). However, female characters were nearly twice as likely to use verbal aggression and ridicule (9% vs. 5% of males), and more than three times as likely to scream (18% vs. 5% of males). In behaviors more traditionally associated with females, they were more than twice as likely as males to share and help (32% vs. 15% of males), and four times as likely to be nurturing (8% vs. 2% of males).

• *Female characters were sometimes hyper-sexualized and male characters were often hyper-muscularized.* One out of every ten female characters (11%) had a very voluptuous body (i.e., very large breasts and a very small waist). Another 7% of female characters had either very thin or extremely disproportionate bodies, meaning that nearly 20% of female characters modeled unhealthy or unrealistic body sizes. In addition, one in three male characters (35%) was extremely muscular.

• *Female sexuality was often accentuated with highly revealing clothing.* Female video game characters showed quite a bit of skin. Nearly one in five female characters (21%) had exposed breasts (7% fully exposed), 13% had exposed buttocks (8% fully exposed), and 20% had exposed midriffs. In addition, females were more than twice as likely as males to wear revealing clothing (20% of females and 8% of males).

• *Males were highly aggressive, and were more likely than females to perpetrate violence without the use of weapons.* Almost two thirds of male characters (63%) engaged in physical aggression, compared to just 40% of female characters. Further, nearly half of males (42%) engaged in hand to-hand combat, compared to 23% of females.

• *Males were three times more likely than females to appear unaffected by violence.* In response to all types of violence, 33% of males appeared unaffected, compared to 10% of females. These differences appear most often in sports games. In cases of non-sports violence, males and females were equally likely (9% and 10% respectively) to be unaffected by violence.

Just as young girls may interpret highly sexualized characters [in video games] as symbols of the "ideal woman," so too may young boys.

Although sexy female characters are created to appeal to males, they can send harmful messages to both male and female players. Just as young girls may interpret highly sexualized characters as symbols of the "ideal woman," so too may young boys. These impressions may influence girls' feelings about themselves and their place in the world, and they may also influence boys' expectations and treatment of females. In both cases, these images can have unhealthy effects on children's self-esteem, behavior and relationships with others.

Equal Opportunity Employers?

While it is becoming more common to see female video game characters in roles traditionally held by males, there is still a tremendous difference in the way males and females are portrayed in these games. Females may be as tough as the males, and may have to face similar missions and opponents, but they have an added challenge: to look sexy while doing it. Following are some examples of the sexual divide between female characters and their male counterparts.

	Male:	Female:
Heroes:	Link in The Legend of Zelda looks like a young boy and is dressed like an elf (complete with tights and pointy hat).	In Tomb Raider, Lara Croft's short shorts and extremely large breasts never keep her from accomplishing her mission.
Soldiers:	Command & Conquer: Red Alert's male soldiers head off to battle in full military gear.	Tanya, Command & Conquer's female GI, battles the Soviets in midriff-revealing tank top and leans forward whenever she speaks to expose her cleavage.
Competitors:	In SSX, male competitors wear the snowboarder's uniform: baggy clothes.	Elise, a female snowboarder in SSX (who is described as 5'11" and 120 lbs.), wears a very tight one-piece snowsuit that shows off her ample bust. When her name is announced for a race, Elise rubs her hands up and down her sides in a very provocative manner.
Guards:	In The Legend of Zelda, the male guard is covered from head to toe in full body armor.	In Final Fantasy IX, the female guard is dressed in an armor brassiere with nothing but a thong to cover her bottom half.
Robots:	Zone of the Enders' male robots have square shaped bodies.	Female robots in Zone of the Enders are quite shapely, with large breasts and curvaceous hips.

10

Video Games Can Be Used for Therapeutic Purposes

Beyond Online Limited

Beyond Online Limited is an affiliate of Beyond 2000, an Australian-based television series that attempts to predict the scientific and technological advances and trends that will shape medicine, computers, space, agriculture, transportation, architecture, entertainment, energy, and the environment.

Video game technology can be used to enhance health. Because video game playing is so appealing, the games can enhance therapies that require a patient's participation. For instance, video games are being used to augment biofeedback therapies—techniques that are used to teach patients to control involuntary body mechanisms—because they require hand-eye coordination. In addition, video games can be used to distract patients from physical pain and reduce levels of stress.

Go shout this news to your parents, partner or colleagues immediately: *video games can be good for you.* They can also be a useful, healing therapy in treating chronic conditions. The proof is in the sick kids that are getting better.

Computer gaming technology can be utilised for medical therapy in two ways: actively and passively. For both approaches though, mind over matter is the key. On the active side of things, for example, there's biofeedback: forcing a normally involuntary body mechanism to behave in a controlled manner. For decades doctors have used biofeedback as a way to help control stress and tension. Now NASA has added a new twist by combining this mental technique with the hand-eye coordination of video games.

As for passive treatments, immersing a patient in a virtual world is a great distraction, taking their focus away from the pain or discomfort they may be experiencing in the physical world. Virtual scenarios have also proven useful for helping people overcome phobias or stress disorders.

Now pay attention 007

According to researchers at NASA's Langley Research Center, specially-designed video games may actually improve and protect a player's mental and physical health. They have developed an interactive system and tested it at Eastern Virginia Medical School (EVMS) in Norfolk, Virginia. The system teaches users to change their brainwave activity or other specific physiological functions while playing popular, off-the-shelf games. This is accomplished by making the video game partially respond to the activity of the player's body and brain instead of just his hands.

"Thirty years of biofeedback research has shown that by training specific brainwave changes, or reductions in other abnormal physiological signals, people can achieve a wide variety of health-enhancing outcomes," said Dr. Olafur Palsson, assistant professor of psychiatry and family medicine at EVMS, and co-inventor of the system. "With this new technology, we have found a way to package this training in an enjoyable and inherently motivating activity."

Wired up like a bad Frankenstein's monster, signals from sensors attached to the player's head and body are fed through a processing unit to a joystick or other game control device. As the player's brainwaves come closer to an optimal, stress-free pattern, the joystick becomes easier to control. This encourages the player to produce those patterns or signals necessary to succeed at the game. By extension, learning how to induce that stress-free state helps players to re-create it away from their games' console when they need it.

Video games can be good for you.

In this way, recreational video games have the potential to help both children and adults with a variety of health problems, from concentration difficulties to physical stress. Unlike earlier biofeedback methods, which tended to be monotonous and simplistic, this technology adapts to today's most popular games, giving players a beneficial side effect, while fully preserving entertainment value.

"This technology is a spin-off of NASA research where we measure the brain activity of pilots in flight simulators," says co-inventor Dr. Alan Pope. "Flight simulators are essentially very sophisticated video games."

In addition, in what could be called a "spin-back" rather than "spin-off" application, NASA is studying ways to use the technology for pilot training.

An effective technique

Early results from a game-based biofeedback study suggest that the technique is effective. In one test, the technology is being applied as a treatment for attention deficit hyperactivity disorder (ADHD). Children with ADHD, between the ages of 9 and 14, either play popular video games or receive more traditional brainwave biofeedback treatment to control their behaviour. Both forms of treatment help the children's symptoms, but the video game approach seems to have distinct advantages.

"The main difference we see between the groups so far is in motivation—the children in the video game group enjoy the sessions more and it is easier for the parents to get them to come to our clinic," says Dr. Palsson.

It's no surprise that children are happy to come along to parentally-approved gaming sessions. For adults though, the fast-paced manipulations of an arcade-style game may not hold much attraction. For that reason other approaches are being investigated by other teams around the world. Doctors at London's Royal Free Hospital have had some success with a biofeedback game treatment for sufferers of irritable bowel syndrome. This largely stress-related illness can cause great abdominal pain.

Specially-designed video games may actually improve and protect a player's mental and physical health.

Hooked up to a polygraph machine, in much the same manner as the NASA system, patients can use their body state to control their progress through a 'virtual bowel'. The 'game' is quite literal, with the players using relaxation techniques to move themselves through red spots of bubbly areas representing bloated pain. Once these obstacles are broken down, the patient emerges into a peaceful country setting with a free-flowing stream, meant to be symbolic of a healthy bowel!

A distraction from pain

Leaving aside all the sensor hook-ups and complex biofeedback interfaces, graphic environments can also help patients on a subtler level. In an Atlanta hospital, children are being fitted out with virtual reality (VR) headsets to take their minds away from their problems.

A report from Associated Press describes the poignant situation of 8-year-old Tyler Callahan, a cancer patient undergoing a chemotherapy regime so painful that his mother used to think the cure was worse than the disease. Pierced by tubes and needles, Tyler was in so much agony at his chemo-sessions that it took two people to hold him down.

A team of researchers decided then to see if they could make Tyler forget the pain by taking away his sight and his attention.

Immersed in VR hardware, Tyler withdraws into a jungle-covered kingdom roamed by mountain gorillas. Twiddling a joystick, Tyler can roam through the rainforest trying to find the digital gorilla troupe and see how close he can get. If he gets too near, a roaring challenge from the alpha-male silverback lets him know where the boundaries are.

The gorilla stalking is such fun and takes so much focus that Tyler's mind begins to lose track of his pain. It won't go away entirely of course, but by not focusing on the discomfort, his stress level is greatly reduced.

Effective addition to counseling

The gorilla game is just the first step in the research and is really only aimed at younger children. However, doctors and technicians at Virtually Better Inc., the developers of Tyler's $4000 system, hope that it will give rise to therapies for older kids and adults, who might be similarly engaged by a rock concert or sporting competition.

Virtually Better is a field leader in using VR for "serious" applications. They have had great success with a virtual plane environment that is used to help people with a fear of flying. In clinical trials it was found to be an effective addition to traditional counseling and limited exposure therapies.

The company even has a "Virtual Vietnam" package designed to help war veterans suffering from post-traumatic stress disorder. With the goggles on, the patient is transported back to the Southeast Asian conflict, zooming low over padi fields and jungle canopy in a virtual Huey helicopter. A separate environment simulates the experience of walking exposed in the middle of an open field surrounded by jungle. Extensive audio effects are incorporated into the setting, controlled by the therapist through keyboard commands. For example, the soundtrack can vary from simple jungle noises through to a full battle including mine detonations, mortars, rockets, small arms fire, screaming, B-52 strikes and helicopters coming in to land.

And if all that combat sounds a bit like a video game, that's because it is. But it's a game with a serious purpose and of benefit to mankind.

Just don't try explaining that to your mum next time you've been caught playing Quake for 12 hours straight.

Organizations to Contact

The editors have compiled the following list of organizations concerned with the issues debated in this book. The descriptions are derived from materials provided by the organizations. All have publications or information available for interested readers. The list was compiled on the date of publication of the present volume; the information provided here may change. Be aware that many organizations take several weeks or longer to respond to inquiries, so allow as much time as possible.

American Psychological Association (APA)
Office of Public Affairs, 750 First St. NE, Washington, DC 20002-4242
(202) 336-5700 • (800) 374-2721
e-mail: public.affairs@apa.org • website: www.apa.org

This society of psychologists aims to "advance psychology as a science, as a profession, and as a means of promoting human welfare." The APA investigates the relationship between violent video games and increased aggression in children. Its publications include "Violent Video Games Can Increase Aggression" and "Children's Personality Features Unchanged by Short-Term Video Play."

Children Now
1212 Broadway, 5th Fl., Oakland, CA 94612
(510) 763-2444 • fax: (510) 763-1974
e-mail: children@childrennow.org. • website: www.childrennow.org

Children Now is an independent, nonpartisan organization whose goal is to improve the quality of entertainment media targeted toward children. It publishes "Fair Play? Violence, Gender, and Race in Video Games."

Computer Addiction Services
McLean Hospital, 115 Mill St., Belmont, MA 02478
(617) 855-2908
e-mail: orzack@computeraddiction.com
website: www.computeraddiction.com

Founded by clinical psychologist Maressa Hecht Orzack, Computer Addiction Services believes that inappropriate computer use is similar to substance abuse. Computer Addiction Services feels that society is becoming more and more computer dependent not only for information, but for fun and entertainment and that this is a potential problem affecting all ages.

iGames
e-mail: info@igames.org • website: www.igames.org

iGames is an organization that believes that in addition to the continuous development of a variety of games, the social environment and interaction provided by game centers is the key ingredient for expanding interactive entertainment to a very diverse and broad community of gamers. The organization has established strong relationships with a broad group of game industry leaders in order to provide a wide variety of products, services and programs to member game centers and video game players. Some of the products and programs facilitated and/or developed by iGames include game community development, exclusive game previews/demos, classes, game launch events, tournaments, and leagues.

Interactive Digital Software Association (IDSA)
1211 Connecticut Ave. NW #600, Washington, DC 20036
e-mail: idsa@idsa.com • website: www.idsa.com

The IDSA is an organization that serves the business and public affairs needs of entertainment software companies. The organization accounts for the majority of entertainment software sold in the United States. In 1994, the IDSA voluntarily established the Entertainment Software Rating Board (ESRB) to review and rate every video game. The ESRB suggests the age appropriateness of games based on the amount of graphic violence, strong language, or provocative themes they contain and has initiated nationwide programs aiming to increase consumer and retailer awareness of the ESRB's rating system.

Interactive Entertainment Merchants Association (IEMA)
64 Danbury Rd., Ste. 700, Wilton, CT 06897
(203) 761-6180 • fax: (203) 761-6184
e-mail: jennifer@iema.org • website: www.theiema.com

The aim of the IEMA is to gather the interactive entertainment industry's leading product retailers together, represent their cumulative wants and needs and address its pressing issues, including the selling of violent video games to young children. The nonprofit association now represents nineteen of the industry's top twenty retailers in the interactive entertainment industry.

International Game Developers Association (IGDA)
600 Harrison St., San Francisco, CA 94107
(415) 947-6235 • fax: (415) 947-6090
e-mail: info@igda.org • website: www.igda.org

The IGDA is an independent, nonprofit organization for video game developers whose mission is to build a community that leverages its expertise for the betterment of the interactive entertainment industry and the development of video games as an art form. The organization's articles include "The Cultural Study of Games: More than Just Games" and "So You Want to Be a Games Designer?," and, it publishes the *IGDA Newsletter*.

The Lion & Lamb Project
4300 Montgomery Ave., Ste. 104, Bethesda, MD 20814
(301) 654-3091 • fax: (301) 654-2394
e-mail: lionlamb@lionlamb.org • website: www.lionlamb.org

The mission of the Lion & Lamb Project is to stop the marketing of violence to children. The project works with parents and other concerned adults to reduce the demand for violent "entertainment" products and with the toy industry and the federal government to reduce the supply of such products. It holds an annual press conference highlighting the year's "Dirty Dozen" violent toys and "Top Twenty" creative nonviolent toys. The Lion & Lamb Project also publishes a newsletter several times a year.

Mediascope
12711 Ventura Blvd., Ste. 440, Studio City, CA 91604
(818) 508-2080 • fax: (818) 508-2088
e-mail: facts@mediascope.org • website: www.mediascope.org

Mediascope is a national, nonprofit research and policy organization working to promote issues of social relevance within the entertainment industry. A principal objective of Mediascope is to encourage responsible portrayals in film, television, the Internet, video games, music, and advertising. The organization publishes *The Social Effects of Electronic Interactive Games: An Annotated Bibliography.*

The National Institute on Media and the Family
606 24th Ave. South, Ste. 606, Minneapolis, MN 55454
(612) 672-5437 • (888) 672-KIDS • fax: (612) 672-4113
e-mail: information@mediafamily.org • website: www.mediafamily.org

The National Institute on Media and the Family, a nonprofit, nonpartisan and nonsectarian organization, is a national resource for research, education, and information about the impact of media on children and families. The institute was created to provide information to parents and other adults about media products and their likely impact on children so they can make informed choices. The mission of the National Institute on Media and the Family is to maximize the benefits and minimize the harm of media on children and families through research and education and does not advocate censorship of any kind. It publishes its findings on video games in the "Video and Computer Game Report Card" and the "Parents' Guide to Video Games."

Bibliography

Books

Bob Bates	*Game Design: The Art and Business of Creating Games.* Indianapolis, IN: Premier Press Books, 2001.
David S. Bennahum	*Extra Life: Coming of Age in Cyberspace.* New York: BasicBooks, 1998.
Van Burnham	*Supercade: A Visual History of the Videogame Age 1971–1984.* Cambridge, MA: MIT Press, 2001.
Justine Cassell and Henry Jenkins, eds.	*From Barbie to Mortal Kombat: Gender and Computer Games.* Cambridge, MA: MIT Press, 2000.
Dave Grossman and Gloria Degaetano	*Stop Teaching Our Kids to Kill: A Call to Action Against TV, Movie, and Video Game Violence.* New York: Random House, 1999.
J.C. Herz	*Joystick Nation: How Videogames Ate Our Quarters, Won Our Hearts, and Rewired Our Minds.* New York: Little, Brown, 1997.
Sue Howard, ed.	*Wired Up: Young People and the Electronic Media.* London: UCL Press, 1998.
Steven L. Kent	*The Ultimate History of Video Games: From Pong to Pokemon—the Story That Touched Our Lives and Changed the World.* Roseville, CA: Prima Publishing, 2001.
Alice Laplante and Richard Seidner	*Playing for Profit: How Digital Entertainment Is Making Big Business Out of Child's Play.* New York: John Wiley & Sons, 1999.
Brenda Laurel	*Utopian Entrepreneur.* Cambridge, MA: MIT Press, 2001.
Mediascope Inc.	*The Social Effects of Electronic Interactive Games: An Annotated Bibliography.* Studio City, CA: Mediascope, 1996.
Mark Pesce	*The Playful World: How Technology Is Transforming Our Imagination.* New York: Ballantine Books, 2000.
Steven Poole	*Trigger Happy: Videogames and the Entertainment Revolution.* New York: Arcade Publishing, 2000.
Marc Prensky	*Digital Game-Based Learning.* New York: McGraw-Hill, 2000.
John Sellers	*Arcade Fever: The Fan's Guide to the Golden Age of Video Games.* Philadelphia, PA: Running Press, 2001.

Periodicals

Hiawaytha Bray — "The Games People Really Play; The Top Ten Video Games Are Probably Not What You Think. And the Players Don't Match the Stereotype, Either," *Boston Globe*, December 10, 2000.

Richard Breyer — "Two Sides of the Screen," *World & I*, October 1999.

Tom Carson — "Head Shot," *Esquire*, July 2001.

Ariana Eunjung Cha — "Game Boy Just Keeps Going; 120 Million Sold in 12 Years, but Long-Term Effects Uncertain," *Washington Post*, May 16, 2001.

Consumer Electronics — "Retailers Toughen Policies," April 16, 2001.

Simon Cooper — "Youths, Guns, and Automatic Responses," *Arena Magazine*, June 1999.

Stephanie Dunnewind — "Child's Play? Parents Can Be Clueless About the Violent Video and Computer Games Kids Are Playing," *Seattle Times*, August 17, 2000.

Dave Grossman — "Teaching Kids to Kill," *National Forum*, Fall 2000.

Lev Grossman — "Play Nation: More than 145 Million Americans Have a Dirty Little Secret: They Play Video Games," *On*, June 1, 2001.

Gale M.B. Hanson — "The Violent World of Video Games," *Insight on the News*, June 28, 1999.

Johnathan Kay — "Defying a Taboo, Nazi Protagonists Invade Video Games," *New York Times*, January 3, 2002.

Robert MacMillan — "Keep Congress Out of the Violence Debate," *Newsbytes*, May 2, 2001.

Tracy McVeigh — "Computer Games Stunt Teen Brains," *The Observer*, August 19, 2001.

Jeffrey Overstreet — "'Not Enough Faith to Convert Enemy,'" *Christianity Today*, August 6, 2001.

Charles Pillar — "Seduced by the Game: Addicts of Online Play Jeopardize Jobs and Personal Lives," *Los Angeles Times*, May 10, 1999.

Edward Rothstein — "Realism May Be Taking the Fun out of Games," *New York Times*, April 6, 2002.

Jacob Sullum — "Violent Reactions," *Reason*, May 19, 1999.

Royal Van Horn — "Technology: Violence and Video Games," *Phi Delta Kappan*, October 1999.

Sharon Waxman — "Click. Bang. It's Only a Game; Video Designers Shrug Off Blame for Teen Violence," *Washington Post*, May 27, 1999.

Christina Wood — "Are Game Machines Hurting Your Kids?" *FamilyPC*, October 2000.

Index

sexism in, 59
struggle vs. violence in, 19–20
therapeutic uses, 65–68
time spent conversing vs. time spent
with, 56
see also violent computer/video games
violence
defined in game rating system, 30,
33–34
in E-rated video games, 31–32, 34
as intrinsic to games, 18
as making a game a struggle, 19–20
in male vs. female characters, 63
as part of human nature, 24
in television, 12, 13
violent computer/video games
artistic use of violence in, 21–22
attack on
first, 32
history of, 24–25
ignorance and, 25–26
channels antisocial impulses in
acceptable way, 24
correlation between aggressive
behavior and, 7–8, 14–16
engaging emotions and intellect in, 58
failure of arresting images in, 20–21
as harmful to children, 12–13

con, 57–58
increase in, 11
leads to real world violence, 7
learning violent behavior and skills
through, 6–7, 14
con, 22–23
as an outlet for anger and frustrations,
8
research needed on, 28
television compared with, 13, 58–59
types of, 11–12, 20
Virtually Better, 68
Virtual Vietnam, 68

Walsh, David, 7–8
war, 24
war games, 23–24
Whole Earth Catalog, 23–24
Wolfstein 3-D, 6
Woods, Tiger, 38

youth
surveyed on video game use, 10
therapeutic uses of video games with,
66–67
video game violence is harmful to,
12–13